Basrayatha

Basrayatha

THE STORY OF A CITY

MUHAMMAD KHUDAYYIR

VERSO

London • New York

First published by Verso 2008
Copyright © Muhammad Khudayyir
All rights reserved

The moral right of the author has been asserted

First published in 2007 by
The American University in Cairo Press
113 Sharia Kasr el Aini, Cairo, Egypt
420 Fifth Avenue, New York, NY 10018
www.aucpress.com

Copyright © 1996 by Muhammad Khudayyir
First published in Arabic in 1996 as *Basrayatha: surat madina*
Protected under the Berne Convention

English translation copyright © 2007 by William M. Hutchins

The epigraph by Éluard on pages 3 and 165 is drawn from Paul Éluard,
"En avril 1944: Paris respirait encore," *Oeuvres complètes* (Paris: Éditions Gallimard, 1968), 1:1297.

The epigraph by al-Sijistani on page 61 is drawn from Abu Hatim
Sahl ibn Muhammad ibn Uthman al-Sijistani, *Kitab al-nakhla* ("Book of the Date Palm"),
Hatim Salih al-Damin, ed. (Beirut: Dar al-Basha'ira al-Islamiya, 2002), 45.

An earlier version of chapter two appeared in *Banipal: Magazine of Modern Arabic
Literature*, no. 26 (Summer 2006).

An abridged translation by Shakit Mustafa of the chapter "Friday's Gifts"
appeared in Muhammad Khudayyir, "Friday's Bounties," *Edebiyat Journal of Middle
Eastern Literature* 13 (1): 69 ff.

Extract from Constantine Cavafy's "The City" from *The Complete Poems of Cavafy*,
trans. Rae Dalven, published in North America by Harcourt Brace Jovanovich and
in the United Kingdom by Chatto & Windus. Reprinted by permission of Harcourt
Brace Jovanovich and the Random House Group Ltd.

Extract from T.S. Eliot's "The Dry Salvages" from "Four Quartets" in *The Complete
Poems and Plays 1909–1962*, published in the United Kingdom by Faber and Faber and
in North America by Harcourt Brace & Company. Reprinted by permission of Faber
and Faber and Harcourt Brace & Company.

The photographs in this book are from the collection of Mu'in al-Mudhaffer.

1 3 5 7 9 10 8 6 4 2

Verso
UK: 6 Meard Street, London W1F 0EG
USA: 180 Varick Street, New York, NY 10014-4606
www.versobooks.com

Verso is the imprint of New Left Books

ISBN 978 1 84467 233 2

British Library Cataloguing in Publication Data
A catalogue record for this book is available from the British Library

Library of Congress Cataloging-in-Publication Data
A catalog record for this book is available from the Library of Congress

Typeset in Perpetua by Hewer Text UK, Ltd
Printed in the USA by Maple Vail

Translator's Acknowledgments

I wish to thank Muhammad Khudayyir for allowing me to translate this important book and for answering questions about it. I also thank Iraqi poet and novelist Fadhil al-Azzawi for answering questions about some words, phrases, and lines of poetry that perplexed me. Part of this translation was created while I held a 2005–2006 grant for literary translation from the U.S. National Endowment for the Arts and an Off-Campus Scholarly Assignment from Appalachian State University. I also thank Sarah, Franya, and Kip Hutchins for being good sports about my translating endeavors.

Contents

Contents

First Exploration

The distance between the city and the man was no longer even a wall's span.

                                                              Paul Éluard

WE HAD NOT yet learned all the nooks of the city where we lived—only our school buildings, the playing field, the nearby river, the garden alongside it, and the neighborhood market. The city was not a place one went to without making preparations and getting help. Later on, though, we began to explore it, bit by bit, in carefree rambles, impetuous raids, or wary excursions. By the time we had learned our way around and come to understand it, we had matured, our legs had grown tired, and our desires had diminished. We no longer felt like leaving our neighborhoods for distant jaunts through the streets. This city had exhausted us, and we no longer had the heart for new discoveries. Today, though, we feel that our knowledge of its secrets has accumulated to such an extent that we cannot keep them from those who come after us. Others—following us—will begin to sweep through it, although they will not reach any hidden location or street our feet did not reach before them. Indeed, they will not even succeed in discovering those places and streets, because the new city extends farther each year, consuming and gutting the old city. Multi-story buildings, tourist hotels, restaurants, entertainment venues, business establishments, and firms rise quickly, and people immediately master all their attractions. What for us was a hard-won knowledge of this city resulting from a cautious, ritualistic series of expeditions into its bowels has today become a normal outing, assimilation, and a crush of humanity engaged in overwhelming, speedy transactions carried out amid a din that rises from every side.

In this chapter, I will describe those first steps, our disorganized excursions, reckless raids, satisfied retreats, and frightened withdrawals: how we explored our city by night and day, in sunshine and in the dark, with avidity and love or hatred, how we felt— fugitive, stealthy, timid, and crude—and how we went: in groups or alone. I will speak on my own behalf, but the narrative of my emotions applies to the others too. I sense that faces are peeking stealthily at my notebook and that figures are skirmishing with each other around my sentences. Fine: I will allot you your due share in these impressions, all you absent friends, whose appearance and names I have forgotten. You are here. So let us begin the excursion and the raid. Do you remember that city?

We used to leave our homes in the outlying regions and head toward the city's heart. Then we would return to our houses early. Later, the distances we traveled from our homes increased day by day. We began to consider ourselves residents of the city, even if we did not know who ruled it, how its institutions functioned, or how the rest of the people lived. The city was developing and expanding without our realizing that this was happening. There were more buildings and people were changing. They would go and return or disappear suddenly. We guessed that situations and events of a frightening, clandestine type were transpiring behind these walls and deep below the earth. There were secrets from which we needed to keep a safe distance. Aliases were concealed behind names publicly displayed on signs by the streets, squares, public gardens, rivers, bridges, markets, cinemas, and neighborhoods.

We entered through many gates, heading in all directions, through the tentacles of darkness and beneath the swords of noonday. These were the city gates and historic arches that raiders and scowling, armed conquerors had breached, carrying within their helmets the plague, syphilis, poisoned amulets, and dark lusts. From their cloaks dust and the scent of spices shook free. From their mouths came barely comprehensible shouts. They advanced down desolate streets that reverberated with the sounds of drawn swords, spurs, and hoof beats. The same city gates through which passed caravans of prophets, pilgrims, slaves, prisoners, migrants, and refugees were those we entered to worship, during epidemics, in times of good fortune and ill. They were open to the rays of sunlight and to sandstorms, to names and dates, and to the declarations and directives posted on them over the course of centuries; we passed through these gates each day and at midnight.

Beneath the gates there were nightmare figures—very dark, with thick beards and mustaches, bristling with weapons—who watched us enter and exit, examining our identities and studying the features of our innocent faces: us, the trembling civilians, workmen, and tramps or beggars, bootblacks, gamblers, prostitutes, agents, thieves, and peddlers. We arrived from the deserts, fields, cemeteries, huts, prisons, quarries, underground vaults, low-ceilinged rooms, damp schools, and narrow lanes—leaving behind us our mothers' kerchiefs and cloaks and our grandmothers' veils, the clothes of our sweethearts, and the shared family bedding. From every cranny and lair we arrived and exited—the innocent, the wretched, and the complacent.

We would pass through the gates, exchange quick greetings, dirty jokes, curses, and smirks—or whisper to one another the password (al-salam alaykum) that we kept on the tip of the tongue as a watch-word or a living charm: everlasting peace with life, the peace that implies a tie to the earth, which we will never quit for any other earth—the word of final demise.

Once had we left the gates we would fan out through the streets and alleyways. Then we would reunite in the corners of the squares and in coffeehouses. We would inspect our faces and limbs and then separate, roaming the streets, our steps regular and following in stride: one step back into the history of an open space, on the highway of a memory forged by thousands of wayfarers before us. Then we marked it by a single echo—that of the tiles of the porticoes, halls, public baths, and hospitals. We would lose one another but soon would be surprised by our faces when we bumped into each other and mingled together, because our faces were spread out through all the neighborhoods, peering down the entries to alleys, at the access points of bridges, at lampposts, market benches, restaurants, gardens, cinemas, boats, and statues. These were relaxed or reserved faces, veiled or unveiled, laughing or distraught.

In that crush of bodies, that human congestion, suspicions could shower people's heads like salt and never reach the ground. We were all in it together, but it was every man for himself. We had impregnable armor that clanked when we collided. Complacent amiability expressed through looks and touches attempted to soften the offense. We withdrew inside our armor and did not interact save with anxious, fleeting glances. Our eyes watched, as though their only occupation was to look—or, as Sartre said, "Their innocent eyes saw me and had no mission save to look at me." Our eyes, though, were not innocent. Those burning eyes, which were dry from excessive staring during insomnia or from shedding tears, showed a terror of unknown dangers and disasters, as well as our suffering, tribulation, questioning, appeal, and entreaty. Similarly, our eyes did not possess the ability to retain for long the images of the world displayed before them, because they cast back the images and scenes before these could be relayed to our leaky, saturated memories. We did not remember the faces of our mates, not even the next day, although we were always crowded together. Each of us told himself, "Whenever I don't see him, he's looking at me." Our eyes colonized nearly identical silent faces. "Amazing! How can faces avoid being importunate and aggressive?" Beautiful faces—ones whose radiance and revelation were provocative—were snatched, cherished, and enslaved in secret, demeaning liaisons: beauty pageants, wedding bonds, sexual slavery, until gradually their radiance was extinguished and buried by the shadows of selfishness and pride, beauty potions and premature aging, or isolation and denial. Then they would soon sink to the status of disgusting, common faces. Neither desperate pride nor daily review would revive the lost youth and specificity of these images and representations.

We would go out to walk, wanting to travel streets that branched out in a random fashion. We would proceed down a long, narrow road that led us to another lengthy road. We would keep on walking in search of other roads, paying no attention to where they led— only to the fact that they continued. We walked without looking at people or the traffic. We focused our attention on our feet and shoes in their progress across the asphalt. Frequently the weather was variable: dusty, humid, rainy, fiery from sunshine, or bleak. We walked as far as the roads' pavement held out beneath our steps, until walls, without any regard to us, blocked the roads, or the roads came to an abrupt end. Walls—high or low—were always setting boundaries for streets, restricting our advance and our choice of destinations. Although we conjectured that the walls concealed special items of furniture, games, and women, we were concerned to see whether their external surfaces were unstained and free of apertures, protrusions, or posters—or stained, patched, and busy with windows and adjacent doors. Even if it had been easy for us to soar over these barriers, we would have been unable to dispense with the walls that left us only narrow passageways that hampered our steps: straight or twisting, short or long, paved or dirt, level or sloping, clean or filthy with garbage and wastewater drains. When roads led us underground through tunnels, the walls were stronger, closer together, and stifling; so we preferred to exit as soon as possible to ground level, where we knew every mystery of the surfaces of our streets' walls.

In the empty spaces of the streets, things were left outside the walls; these seemed more human and real because they were exposed to daily view, contact, and use. There were posters, wheelchairs, poles, barrels, and porters' pads. Their shapes and locations were defined by their relationship to us or our relationship to them. Without our attention, they would have been pointless, tossed into storage or out into the sun, wind, and rain to perish.

We could hear the groans of items held prisoner by walls as they moved, or their profiles would thrust up high enough to be visible from roofs or windows: bedsteads that dreams had smashed, chairs destroyed by relaxation, cups that lips had rubbed smooth, dead stoves, and aged dolls.

Without meaning to, some of us would walk directly behind someone else, hot on the trail of the human scent—as if under the influence of a magnetic attraction. Once the streets were deserted, the luminous vestiges of those who had disappeared drew our attention. When we were totally lost, the streets would lead us wherever they were heading. We would spread out in an alarming fashion. The drivers of vehicles could scarcely keep from hitting one of us. Even when we were by and large confined to a sidewalk, they would run over our shadows, which extended beyond the curb to the far side of the street.

We made a point of examining our reflections in mirrors, shop windows, pictures, and newspapers. Similarly, we had secret monikers and nicknames. Our images would merge and one would disappear into another till we barely recognized ourselves. During our hours of wandering, we would lose track of our human existence; we were simply walking. That was because there were streets and places that accommodated us and led us by our reins. That was because there was a space that catered to our obedient humanity, which we risked losing at the slightest error; how many errors denied us our manhood and how many chance occurrences offered it back to us.

We entered the city one morning only to find it a desert bombarded by a sun that was closer to the earth than ever before. We sought refuge from its midday heat in the shade of the walls, although its fire pursued us and scorched our heads. It seemed to us that the buildings were about to melt in the flame of that weird day. It was a day of pestilential moonlight, a day of upheavals, a day of gunfire, a day of suicide, a day of death, a day of collapse, a day of rejection, and a day to end all days.

Debilitated and wary, we watched the hazy shadows of our bodies as these collided with solid entities. They fell like corpses, took on different shapes and then were penetrated by doors and openings. They blew futilely on cold ashes, merged with each other, underwent metamorphoses or disappeared, bowing humbly, advancing at a crawl, collapsing submissively, shooting off angrily, hesitating contemptuously, becoming smooth and transparent in affectionate and dreamy moments, and splintering and blowing away like dust when we felt regretful, shamefaced, and resigned. We observed ourselves as our spirits drifted over the flames, escaping from us as we incredulously bid them farewell and they vanished in the stillness of those long days.

Even so, we were the lords of the day each Friday, during the vigorous, noonday heat. We were the chosen beings, sporting green, reeking of rotting onions; our words were devoid of hope, although they were injurious and as rough as stones. We pelted each other with heartless, improvised phrases—delivered quickly or dragged out in the passages of the ancient souks—from teetering coffeehouse benches and the seats of crowded restaurants. Each radiant Friday, the lords of the day began their crowded review by unleashing a day of judgment on this world: an interrogation of the errors of a fellow citizen, his vulgarity and careless abuse of ethical norms—carried out with an all-consuming desire and with spiritual distress, as one probed another with a flurry of inquiries. On encountering an old friend, one would start with questions about status, family, and the yield of the new season. From the familiar shop, to a mausoleum, to a coffeehouse, they carried with them on their sandals and clothing the smell of the earth, of roots, and of tobacco. The cloaks of their women put in an appearance at the entries of souks and at the tombs. These cloaks exuded the scents of herbs, milk, dung, medicines, and wool fabrics. After overrunning, penetrating, wheeling about, and tottering in fatigue through souks displaying textiles, tobacco products, fish, vegetables, ropes, and fragrances respectively, after sucking greedily from the day's teat, they would turn their ears to the noontime call to prayer from the surrounding minarets. It would sweep aside conversations and spread carpets of silence through the thickets of the markets. The electric sound of radios would die, cash would disappear, the hands of watches dangling from silver chains would unite, and the sparkle of gems in rings would go out.

Hopes and greedy desires would be postponed, and ritual ablution would commence inside the courtyards of brick mosques at low-set spigots, in preparation for the noon prayer. Then the masters of the day would prostrate themselves under the weight of inherited sins. Even so, a single hour sufficed to cleanse their spirits. After that, they spread out in regions where the day had begun to shrink and withdraw its blessings. They finally felt the extinction of Friday's gifts and, little by little, despair and depression, which would haunt them throughout the remainder of the day, would settle in their souls.

The gods, demons, and sorcerers, heroes and inventors, thieves and prostitutes, sentries and aliens, ghosts and victims, the demented and the deformed: all came out at night. They would awaken to the bells hanging from the vast fringes of darkness and begin their extensive circuit. No night anywhere rivals our pitch-black, gorgeous, southern night. In our consciousness this night exists throughout the day beneath its surface, in our hearts, songs, eyes, and the ink of our pens. Our night belongs to a special type of Asiatic night—a youthful one, like a powerful, dark, calm, daring boy—a night that once displayed atmospheric games for prehistoric jungles. This great night attempts to enclose us in a single square and then to scatter and pursue us to the doors of our houses following the cinema's final show and the closing of the last coffeehouse. All the same, the nightly game motivates us to escape from the night's soft grasp and to pursue our aimless wanderings.

In the gloomy recesses of crooked backstreets and alleys that split off in a labyrinth from the darkened city center, with faces secretly drained by alienation and loneliness, brooding and terror, submission and humiliation, beneath walls in the darkness, we drag the plume of our feet and the flowers of our bodies and their fruits, which are heavy with seeds and pollen. We are stuffed, heavy, staggering. Our craving lacks a target, a conscience, or a desire. Our steps are covert and our heads confused. For an instant, eyes meet in the dark, and we discover our pallor, bafflement, and confusion—we are brothers in misery and despair.

We advance along the night's arteries as the city vanishes together with its lights and colors. Only calm, still houses remain, with fathers, mothers, and sisters tucked inside them; mankind is a group of strangers. Then here or there, unexpected banquets and discreet weddings welcome us. We reach the outer limits of phantom shrines, tombs, and spectral gardens. I can still remember the night's phosphorescent specters and the nocturnal spirits' canvases, which were displayed in secret museums.

Red: empty streets, bridges, posters, martyrs, and the slaughter-house.

Yellow: desert dawn and an exile of waiting.

Green: gardens without children, and a pallet made to hold an entire family.

Black: a funeral, domino, and iron chains.

White: days, noons, and chalk.

Gray: ancient cities, ruins, and storms.

Blue: amulets and domes.

Pale yellow: cholera, malaria, and hotel beds.

Black again: 'Travel Prohibited' signs, prisons, rifles, and bitumen-coated reed boats.

White again: a cup, the public bath, and a shroud.

Red again: bilharzia.

Green again: floods and lakes.

Black again: the railroad, night stations, and mothers.

Brown: doors, balconies, sandals, rebecs, and henna.

Gold: mosques, anklets, and hunger.

Lemon: the moon and the eyes of patients with jaundice.

We attempted to flee from the night's museums. Outside, the night changed into a huge insect with many legs, crawling forward at an imperceptible pace. Our paths led us to the fringes of the swamps, to huts resembling bird nests. Our feet would creep forward beneath the fog of the insect's dewy body. We would smell its breath, which mingled with the scents of rice, alcohol, offal, incense, and henna. We listened to the continuous grinding inside it: drums, chains, whips, and shears. The insect would make a whistling hiss that stirred up the dust of the pavement, took plaster off the walls, shook the leaves of trees, and agitated the dogs, so that their barking and howling increased.

We proceeded forward but ultimately reached the night's final boundary: another swamp, a brothel, or our own cold beds.

In children's imaginations, the city is the workplace that fathers leave when they return home, a souk mothers frequent for shopping, and a school for brothers. What they do not know are the terrifying insect's frightful guts, submerged in the dark.

The images that streamed through our heads brought a noise like the hiss of steam when life—which had been jammed into limbs—attempted to escape. We walked calmly, alertly, with dignity and humility, with steps that were unsteady or spiritless—while we tried to restrain those members from slipping away like water going over a fall. To this end we made an effort to delay our innards' explosion till the last possible moment. We would come face to face with the doors of our houses and knock with impatient fatigue or place the key in the lock indignantly. Inside, waiting up for us, would be yawning faces, chairs, mirrors, and books, as well as the body pertaining to us, the one for which we were responsible, until the following day.

At midnight, the hour for slinking away, for prowling, for desolation—twelve feeble strokes inside our chests—our spirits led their excursion to an end. Behind us were forsaken bits of debris laid to rest in public gardens, the nooks of houses, and on the benches and deserted seats of coffeehouses. The incoming moan merged with the sound of the sentries' whistles and the song of the night's belching insect. We listened carefully: a single, earthy chant proceeded stealthily from the night's expanse, its heart open, beyond the city's hills—a monotonous, uncanny snore.

Night brought together the names of the undocumented, statues, the wood, knockers, and nails of doors, corpses, sentries, beggars, and the driver of the last vehicle—in a profound hour when the insect of the night reached the restricted zone where sentries with long rifles pursued the dead and the murdered, the police chased wild dogs, and misery haunted the nightclub singer.

We moved out in the humid dawn, which was destined to be short-lived, and which rose from the waterways and spread like a cloak to encompass all the beings out at first light: yawning laborers, loitering beggars, rushing soldiers, vigorous women selling milk, and dogs sniffing the ground and wading into ponds.

Once more motions, inclinations, and names awakened blood, nerves, fingers and guts. From the far side of closed doors and windows were heard murmurs, the cries of an infant, and the slosh of dishes being washed. Similarly, we heard behind them muffled sounds for which we struggled to imagine the source: a fire being lit, a coverlet pulled back or spread across a bed, nursing, defecating, milk's froth spilling over, someone chewing, sipping, or kissing, and drowsy words.

Dawn: gray life emerging from a cracked egg, the heavy air sweeping the streets, preparing for a new day. The roads were moistened by the dew, and the umbrellas of traffic cops ballooned like mushrooms, even though the street lights still shone.

The residue of the night: carts fastened with chains, coffeehouse benches, garbage cans, locks, shop posters, and a beer can. . . . A speeding car passed, shredding dawn's equilibrium and gray chastity.

There were successive calls and greetings. The cloak was ripped by knives that fell from the sky, which suddenly revealed itself, and here were the pupils, who carried leather satchels, heading to their schools.

Umm al-Brum
Banquet in a Cemetery

The street spills into the square
At dawn. Then the coffeehouse manager counts his money
And, behind the counter, the waiter washes glasses.
When an automobile speeds through the square
An aged beggar opens his eye
To curse the driver.

Kathim al-Hajjaj

T HE CITY CHANGES the names of its neighborhoods the way it
changes the names of its natives, in order to join everything in
a single current, emerging from its historic womb. It sacrifices bits
of a name to save the whole, in order to diminish childbirth's pains,
time's extension, and the map's disfigurement. One area, for example,
was a cemetery for the poor and then a square named in honor of
King Ghazi. Next, it took the ancient, maternal name: Umm al-
Brum, since the square was like an umbilical cord for the city. The
winding market had numerous names: Souk al-Maghayiz, the Indian
Souk, or the Apothecaries Souk. Those born during the British
occupation from 1914 to 1941, however, forget today those
aforementioned, contentious, heterogeneous stages that affected the
souk and took hold of the square with its jargon, spices, merchandise,
and rifles. They do not countenance anything beside the square's and
the market's present appearance, the true character of which is
revealed late at night. They ignore the past, which endures in wooden

19

balconies, where bats hide in crevices. In total silence they study the hundreds of placards hung along the narrow passageway that leads to the square. These bear the names of current and bygone physicians' clinics, pharmacies, goldsmiths, boutiques, vendors of spices and sweets, restaurants, bakeries, coffee shops, and barbers. Names and logos refer to ancient bones that malaria devastated or that in their youth the sea's swordfish slew. The souk pours into the square the juice of its names, its most recent song. Then it comes to rest, exhausted. This square is the last place to fall asleep and the first to awake. The tired city slowly returns to it. Then quickly dawn's workers occupy it, rousing the ancient market. The other markets yawn and join it.

Another image that has stuck in the memory of those born during the British occupation is that of the first days of the 1958 Revolution. The souk was so crowded then with bodies packed together in a spontaneous procession that it seemed an alley that led from a world of bondage and gloom to a square of freedom and light. After this great day, the square never presented such a unified visage again, for it was poisoned day and night by appropriations and by subsequent vicissitudes.

Call it the city's heart; say it is the city's head, brain, or subconscious. Call it the city's stomach, its urinary tract, round flat foot, or arm supporting its buildings. Say the square is the city's eyes and the perceptive pupils its past. Say the square is the city's clock, counting the seconds of its future; that it is the city's table and bedstead, its banquet and pallet. Say the square is its cellar, its stream of consecutive dreams over the ages. The square is the center where souks strew their refuse, backs cast down their loads, and shoulders relinquish their history. Here are most of the city's restaurants and coffee shops, for it is a communal belly. Here are the city's oldest places of entertainment. The square was the city's first dance floor. Here is the oldest tavern, for the square is the city's final intoxication. Here was the first cinema. Its wide, informative façade towered over the human thread that passed outside its consciousness. Here was the oldest public toilet, the oldest fire station, the oldest brothel. Here one found the largest collection of bootblacks, newspaper vendors, drunkards, and lottery-ticket dealers—along with the longest line of noisy day laborers. Here was the station for half of the city's taxis, serving as the hub of the city, providing circulation between the limbs, blood, sweat, and members of the city's body. Here were the largest post office and the highest communications tower, linking nerves and words in a unified, flowing message. Here you find the roar followed by the whisper, the guffaw and then a rattling in the throat, the storm and then the calm. Hands, arms, cunts, and perplexed faces . . . brains buffeted by songs, numbers, and other stimuli; the physical world followed by the supernatural, followed in turn by total amnesia, even though some original portions of the square remain visible. The imaginative reel at the square's cinema, however, brings to light—in a darkness like the tomb's— images that are extracted from it to assume bodily shape on the living screen. For this reason, the square is the longest thread in the city's subconscious and in the subconscious of the four poets from the 1950s, who filled the Iraqi night with singing and bellowing, with vagrancy, illness, and death. You all know them; names are of no importance. Names are held prisoner in the square by poetry's demons, who were as informal as their odes, which lacked names, addresses, and a past. How their forms changed! How their features aged or slipped from sight! Let us agree to abbreviate all these names into only one, just as the owners of the bars in those days all shared a single name: Hanna.

I look at the square—Umm al-Brum—as an urban scab, continually swelling up and then subsiding. Skin grows like a story rising atop the lower story of the square's subconscious. I noticed, back when public toilets lined its wall, that its normal employment as a square was organically linked to creation and decay. I entered its walls when it was a cemetery confined by the Khandaq and Ashar rivers. I looked to it as a homeland for superstitious tales of hunger. It played host to émigrés, refugees, and wayfarers, whom it fed from giant kettles set on open fires beneath slender palms. I observed the mingled fragments of cloths that had once covered bodies—the remnants of shrouds, tattered rags, and coffins. I listened to the decay of obliterating tombs, the sucking of cooked bones, the smacking of broth and sopped bread, and the chewing of kernels of bulgur. From one banquet to the next, the cemetery's subconscious is supplied with new information by the whispering of reporters, the jokes of buffoons, the murmurs of migrants, the hymns of dervishes, and the hallucinations of the deranged. Behind each kettle stood a wealthy benefactor, the proprietor of orchards, or a woman who had made a vow. Before each cauldron was an army of the creeping destitute. From one year to the next, through epidemics, famines, and wars, one of the layers of the dead in the cemetery turns over to relate a chapter about an extraordinary and unprecedented banquet. Here I transmit a story that has come to me from the world of the dead.

We are in the year 1831, the year of the greatest plague, on the gloomy fall night when town criers announced—with mizmars and drums—the lifting of the plague after it had dealt a fatal blow to half the inhabitants of the city. The residents, who were hidden behind the heavy, bolted doors of their houses, heard the drumming and fearfully peeked out to investigate the patter of returning footsteps of those who had fled the city or the creaking wheels of the iron crematory that volunteers pulled through the alleys during the days of the plague. Those returning to the city knew nothing of this mobile crematory, which the night's narrators had transformed into disquieting rumors that imprisoned in cellars beneath their houses those citizens unable to flee. People who arrived by the sea route from the Gulf regions approached the lifeless, walled city by the river fort and the ships moored before it, while clouds of smoke billowed above them. Then they disembarked within view of the captain, who was standing behind the window in the fort and in the line of fire of soldiers—whose ranks, mustaches, finger rings, and guns were directed over the wall. Silence reigned as metallic objects like the links of the ships' chains rusted. There were no draft animals or carts awaiting the returning people, because the Basrans had eaten all the horses and mules during the plague. They spent their night in the shadow of the fort and did not hear a single dog bark or a cock greet the dawn. The river's winds spread through the exhausted city the smell of burnt clothing and furniture and the scent of garlic, which the survivors had eaten to ward off the disease. Dusk fell quickly and the scattered firing of the night patrol resounded before a feeble call to evening prayer issued from the minaret of the al-Maqam mosque. One man from among the returning people who had sought shelter in the mosque had issued the call. Then a string of minarets—towering over the city's rooftops—answered with a wave of calls to prayer that reached the ears of the refugees at the fort. These sounded to them like the last sigh of the convalescent body of the city as it remembered its casualties and its scattered citizens. Fugitive life returned. The lanterns in the governor's palace and on the main streets were lit. Even so, darkness reigned in the merchants' coffeehouse, in the tobacco market, in the empty grain warehouses, in deserted neighborhoods, and in the cemetery. The river led new returnees to their homes, where their neighbors greeted them with a joy tinged with terror. In the pervasive silence, cannon fire rang out from the river fort. This was the sole signal the governor could use to invite the inhabitants of his city to a dinner planned for the square adjacent to his residence. The invitation did not reach all the residents until the mizmar-and-drum corps appeared in the alleyways in a clangorous parade. Survivors of the plague poured into the palace square, which was illuminated by lanterns placed at intervals and by the open fires over which were set large kettles redolent of cooking food. Hungry recluses, the lame, and the blind gathered, but not a cat or a dog was to be seen. People began slowly and coldly at first to become reacquainted, but then neighbors, associates, and friends found each other fondly and emotionally. Those who had died were dead. Those who had survived were alive at this ultimate moment when staggering bodies embraced and eyes met after being dimmed by lengthy seclusion or dulled by fear, waiting, and hunger. On subsequent nights, a battalion of strangers poured into the site. Tucked beneath their cloaks were parcels of colored garments. The banquet lasted for three nights. The governor—disguised by a cloak, a hat, and a veil that hid his mustache and beard—strolled among the hungry folk. He was accompanied by his Armenian treasurer, who was also disguised—as a hunchbacked beggar. By the light of the lantern that the Armenian aide held, they examined the emaciated faces and predatory fingers that clutched the food or wiped greasy lips. Of all the carnal appetites and lusts only that for food survived. The night watch pretended not to notice the quarrels and clamor, because they had witnessed something craftier, crueler, and more amazing than this brawling and unrest. Meanwhile the glances of the governor's probing eyes stripped people's bones and skulls bare of their incongruous rags, and his ears plucked snuffles, whispers, and smackings from lips and teeth. All the parts would need to be put back together and the citizens' spirits and hearts overhauled. The governor, with what he had left of his imagination, was sketching new roads, hospitals, coffee-houses, theaters, public baths, and mosques. He was also searching through the ragtag returnees for one man who was nowhere to be found among the laborers, cupbearers, butchers, blacksmiths, builders, teachers, and mosque imams. Then he turned to his aide and instructed him to return life and vitality to everything the city had lost. The treasurer understood that his master wished him to arrange to have the air freshened and perfumed in the damp state-rooms on the courtesans' ship in the harbor, in the smoking wing of the balcony of the coffeehouse on the shore, and in the music court in the amusement park. The governor's final request was: "First, though, find that amazing man . . . what do you call him?" The aide answered cautiously, "The storyteller? He suffered a misfortune, master. He was killed. The guards mistook him for a thief and opened fire on him. Master, you know how chaotic things were then." The governor repeated his demand, "Search for another storyteller then; the tales must continue, treasurer."

The second storyteller died in the famine of 1871. The third died with the arrival of the British occupation forces in 1914. Fortunately the fourth—and possibly the last—storyteller lived until the year

25

of the second occupation in 1941. Thus our fathers heard him discuss the communal banquets that were transferred to the cemetery on the city's western outskirts. The storytelling continued with the banquets.

The following tale was recited twice, once in the muleteers' caravansary, which is near the customs office, and once in the coffeehouse adjacent to the cemetery wall, where the draft animals were tethered in the stable after a trip from the city to the cemetery. During its first telling, the mule drivers themselves formed the audience. They were resting on a winter night during 1914 in this caravansary, which smelled of wheat, rice, tobacco, fish, and camphor. Those were days of relaxation and unemployment after the grain warehouses had been plundered but also days when funeral parties were conveyed by draft animals to the cemetery. In one of the caravansary's halls, the teamsters listened to what had happened to the chief muleteer during the chaos that followed the entry of the British into the port of al-Faw and their advance along the river through its farms. The narrator repeated news of the customs employees who had carried away sacks of liras as they withdrew with the Ottoman army from Basra, leaving the customs warehouses open to the city's rabble and to the tribal cavalrymen who had come to the Turks' assistance only to turn their attention to plundering the vaults of the money changers, the warehouses of the merchants, and the homes of the officials who had fled. Police officers disappeared from the streets, which filled with the wounded, thieves, mules, and dogs, as the artillery approached the city and harbingers of the invasion were carried along the sixty-three miles of the Shatt al-Arab's waters: refuse, clothing, fezzes, corpses, and stray skiffs. The winds carried the scent of gunpowder and blood. Far removed from this orgy of terror and booty, the robust chief muleteer leaned against the wall of the cemetery, blinded, his hair and nails ablaze, his skin scorched, as if he had encountered the inferno of a blast furnace.

The audience for the second telling of our story was a mixed group of teamsters, foreigners, cemetery visitors, and gravediggers, and the new narrator—a dirt-covered gravedigger—added new details to the incident of the murder of the leader of the teamsters' guild: "He met his death in exactly the same manner as the second storyteller. I saw him. I buried him." The gravedigger, who resembled a bony specter molded from tombstone dust as he performed one of his terrifying roles, tossed out words as if tossing dirt into a grave: "They ascertained that our muleteer was none other than the third storyteller, and it's difficult to get hold of men like that. Instead of dying like normal people, they are struck by lightning, so that their tongues are roasted in their mouths." In this way, the focus of the narrative was redirected toward the man's frightening demise. On that cold day in December, while the imperial forces spread through the defenseless city, they prepared for the decisive, disjointed battle. "What did you fools know about him? Nothing. So let me tell you some things you don't know about your comrade." The screening for candidates—whether teamsters, gravediggers, or others—for the position of third storyteller was taxing, because in those times the storyteller was normally someone who concealed his gift beneath a menial day job. Once night fell, his second identity crept out in search of a story he could later recount to patrons of the caravansaries, souks, coffeehouses, baths, and the cemetery. Being a gravedigger was also a front for many other employments, and the mattock was merely his tool and emblem—for digging and for plotting—as we shall see. Now he was speaking about the multiple faces of his rival, who had been a teamster by day.

The dead teamster, the son of one of the city's wealthy families, had squandered his funds in dancehalls and in the bedchambers of women entertainers. When he ended up at the teamsters' caravansary, he possessed only some perfumed souvenirs of a final passionate infatuation with the body of a dancer from Aleppo called Nurhan. She had chained him by the neck with a thread of Parisian perfume before he was shackled to his donkey with a noose of flatulence. On that cold night in November, he was seared by fiery, pure-scented breezes that came from a large residence for dancers—adjacent to a casino. He hopped on his mount and hastened there only to find that the hand of destruction had preceded him, assailing the elegant residence. The wind of emptiness whistled through the courtesans' deserted cubicles. A lecherous Indian raid had emptied the coffers of their beautiful, petite treasures but had left him his Aleppine sweetheart, naked among torn pillows, shattered mirrors, and spilled drinks. She had slipped between the sheets, which were damp with viscous liquids, and was raving about the loss of her jewelry, soap, and perfume. Finally she calmed down under the gnawing weight of the nightmare, which was imprinted on her weeping eyes. The gravedigger recounted how he had received the dancer's body, which the teamster carried on the back of his donkey and deposited in a pit in the cemetery. The following night, the roasted teamster was discovered by the wall. "He was scented with perfume as if he had been stewed in a cauldron of rose water." The gravedigger had composed his story's end, from which the era of the fourth storyteller begins.

Next came tales of hunger and of storytellers' bones found by the wall of the cemetery. The iron crematory, which kept advancing, arrived to consume the last of the bones. Late one night, the fourth storyteller witnessed the terrifying crematory, which was drawn by chains attached to a huge chassis that moved with a frightening persistence. He heard the scraping of its couplings before the sound of the oven's blaze. It was no secret that the four storytellers fell as strangers, unrecognized, by the blazing walls of the night. They had been following the legend of the crematory through the previous centuries and—just when they were on the verge of uncovering its secret—were smelted by the inferno of its greedy cavity. The demise of the fourth storyteller occurred during the summer of 1941 amid chaos comparable to that of previous wars. Fortunately, however, he was able to compose the ending of the story of the cemetery before he died—as was revealed through one of the gravedigger's secret guises. The third storyteller had discovered this, but then it caused his death. The gravedigger was actually a moneychanger, who speculated on currency swings during crises and upheavals, trading gold liras for banknotes. The stock exchange of the dead increased after each epidemic, occupation, flight, and theft. The fourth storyteller—before his demise—reported that there were ten huge jugs of Ottoman Mejidi liras and an equivalent amount of assorted currencies in jugs lined up in a cellar beneath the tombs. In that bank in the ground, the gravedigger filled each jug with a special type of coin: the Ottoman lira, the rial, shami, piaster, toman, or rupee. No one revealed the existence of this treasure. The fourth storyteller claimed that the municipal workers who did away with this cemetery in 1933 discovered the jugs and transferred them to a municipal building. Perhaps he was on the trail of the treasure when he collided with the mobile crematory, which smelted him on that ill-omened night— just as it had smelted his predecessors.

The municipal council turned its attention to the Umm al-Brum cemetery in 1933—ignoring the protest of its trustees and

correspondence from the provincial government—and obliterated
the tombstones and the public toilets next to them. It also replaced
the ancient wall with a wooden fence enclosing a cultivated tract
irrigated by a pump, which drew water from the Khandaq River.
The oldest photograph taken of that new green layer goes back to
those early years. At the center of the picture was a circular umbrella
beneath which a policeman directed the day's traffic. Then, when it
was dark, his place was taken by a spectral arm that sundered the
garden's green curtain and directed the destinies of the traffic at
night, seizing souls to their depths. The night drew workers from
the grain warehouses out of their huts of reed mats on the bank of
the Khandaq and propelled wayward men and women from the
houses of al-Ashar to the square, where they assembled around the
umbrella, which extracted from the lowest classes a new superstition.
Thus the banquets continued: funerals for children and unidentified
corpses, for occupation troops, the 1930 accord, the plundering of
the grain warehouses in 1941, the demonstrations and celebrations
for revolutions, the 1964 funeral for al-Sayyab, public hangings,
mobilizations of military vehicles in the following wars, foreign
workers (Egyptians, Sudanese, Somalis), food vendors' carts, bootblacks, taxicabs, street singers, gambling backgammon players:
brethren by day and confederates by night. I do not know when the
emaciated chassis will grow tired of furnishing the tale-spinner with
a phonograph record—a revolving disc that never finishes providing
food, money, or dialogue—or when it will disintegrate beneath the
harsh summer sun. We have a date with our poets, newborns,
warriors, and captives at another banquet.

There is no way to offer a representation of the square arranged
according to events copied from its evolving history, which, as I

picture it, is a chain of nighttime excursions, luminous signs that succeed each other on a darkened screen. For that reason, we will begin our excursion with the nearby al-Hamra' cinema, later known as the sepulchral Karnak. We—those of us who were born during the years of the occupation—would sit with the four poets in our voyeurs' seats, spying on life as it was constituted by a beam of rays from behind our heads. I can find no analogy for it more appropriate than bone dust. The faint hum of the projector's two reels was remarkably similar to the rustling of shrouds passing through Umm al-Brum's gate, where a lantern's weak light glimmered.

We observe through holes of silence, darkness, and coldness a shared film of sunny days. We are surprised between one presentation and the next by clips of a smuggled sex film, but between the convulsions of our peeping senses, we obtain the true sinew that extends through the life of the lost odes and a stanza of the one-name-fits-all poets of the fifties. One day I discovered that sinew among the seats of the bottom section of the cinema. That film was the basis for my story "Night Trains," which is a poetic account of the train coaches that jolted our spirits between desert stations. The empty seats in the movie theater had been filled by the merging spirits of the four poets. I felt their existence every time I heard a protracted sigh like the solution of a stranger's perplexity or a muffled cry of alarm that escaped startled people when the mice racing beneath the seats collided with their feet. That day they were watching their footing or their rain-soaked, loose-fitting overcoats as they entered the Habash coffee shop or left it for The White Rose bar. Heavy rain was falling on ships in the Gulf and the river, on smuggling boats traversing the Shatt al-Arab, friends in prison, and date thieves hiding in the dense riverside papyrus thickets. Dealers

were returning with the scrap metal they had purchased, prostitutes
and housewives were fighting off sleep in their unpretentious houses
and private retreats, respectively, but the poets were reciting their
odes in a cold tavern around a table bolted to the floor. They were
sipping white arrack and savoring salted slices of cucumber, hot
chickpeas, and pomegranate kernels. Burial grounds lay open before
their dances, sails were filled by legends and wilted flowers, and
hemistichs poured out in succession in elaborations free of the chains
of meter, wealth, or abode. On a dark night that besieged the tavern's
lamp with the tremors of desires, the poet with Jaykur's features,
which distinguished him from his companions, recited the first draft
of his poem "Umm al-Brum" while dreaming of a salon packed with
drinks, ladies, magnificent clothes, and promises of international
renown. His voice traveled beyond the tavern's walls and the square,
preceding him to the hospital, where from his bed he would write
the poem "The Stone Mattock" after years of sitting in a Basra tavern.
Two voices met there: a sorrowful rural voice and that of a displaced
alien. These voices returned together along with the corpse that fell
on the pavement of Umm al-Brum, near the site of the tavern, on
a bleak, cloudy evening in the sixties.

I saw the caravans of the living, journeying from their abodes,
Pursued through the night by the lanterns' specters.
I heard the sobbing of their mourner,
The scream of their infant, the thirsty bleating of their livestock,
And, in the glare of midday, singing in pain, someone calling out,
"O Driver of the buff camels,"
But I did not see the dead, whom the gravedigger was expelling
From the old pits, stripping them of shrouds or covering them;

But I did not see the dead before your moist earth dislodged them;
A city's impudence, a dancer's song, and a bartender;
As though your red roses were a lifeless coal,
As though your earth, Umm al-Brum, was shaken by disgrace.*

The sixties brought the demolition of the tavern, coffeehouse, fire station, and cinema, and the area of the square filled with the cooing of gray ringdoves and the scent of pollen.

Even so, the loudest call the four poets heard was the mariner's that the steamships released as they left the harbor. The friends went their separate ways. Then their aging ghosts returned individually to the square, for the banquets did not end with the death of the Jaykur poet. It was necessary for an inn to be established along the side of the square to welcome the returning specters of the poets each year on a predetermined night in February, together with those who had been killed in the Iran-Iraq War of the 1980s. The reunions in the hotel continued throughout the war years. They reached their apex during a thrilling night subsequent to the violent attack on al-Faw in 1986 when the Jaykur poet recited to deceased ancestors and war casualties his threnody, which had until then been implicit in his voice. I was in the square collecting documents relative to the annual banquet honoring the return of the past's scholars, poets, and warriors when I was directed to that isolated hotel, which stood at the edge of the square. I borrowed the sign at its portal—"Sages' Residence"—for use in my story "The Three Sages."†

(A) indicates the author's footnotes; (T) indicates the translator's footnotes.

* The opening lines of "Umm al-Brum" by Badr Shakir al-Sayyab, although the last two lines included here do not appear in the version of this poem in his collected works: Badr Shakir al-Sayyab, *Diwan* (Beirut: Dar al-'Awda, 1971), 1:130–31. (A/T)
† Muhammad Khudayyir, *Ru'yat kharif*, 17–27. (T)

I doubt that my sign will lead you to this hostelry, assuming that it still hangs among the signs for the other small hotels that surround the square with their wooden balconies or that are tucked down its alleys. I returned to the residence's location four years later and found that a wretched hotel had swallowed the hall used for the sages' banquet and that this space was filled with bodies for a different banquet. Any entryway of these hotels with painted facades, toward the end of the night, will accommodate four or five heaps of bodies stretched out in a mass, drawn by the location's warmth and proximity both to the street and to dreams of the cemetery. Those who have sought shelter in the court of the hotel are the square's boys, who shine shoes, sell cigarettes, and act as automotive dent-repair specialists. They are returning from the day's outing, left behind by a family's migration, or fugitives from the streets' violence. I will not claim that this scene of sleeping children is a more or less accurate portrayal than those in Dickens's *David Copperfield* or Mahfouz's *Khan al-Khalili*, but it is palpable, so that the original, realistic truth cannot be compared with the truth of today. This is a predatory scene wrested from the womb of the city, which presents each evening on the cemetery's carpet a fresh banquet for the night's hunters and the metallic crematory. I am also not confident that the ghost of the Jaykur poet returns to this hostelry, but his enthusiastic, trembling voice as he recites "Weapons and Children" makes the young angels, with immature wings, fall asleep, al-Ashar's dogs that follow him lie down, and the ancient residences lean forward and block the alleys with their balconies.

This is not the end of the film, for the two reels of the square's subconscious continue revolving beneath the surface over which today creep pedestrian and vehicular traffic—oblivious to the secret banquets of the cemetery. We finish a reel and return the take-up reel, which has filled automatically. I have similarly composed my story about these banquets in "language more secretive than the gloom of the forest"* for the dead and the living alike.

---

* A phrase from the poem "Umm al-Brum" by Badr Shakir al-Sayyab, *Diwan*, 1:133. (A/T)

Shatt al-Arab
A River's Dream

I do not know much about gods; but I think that the river
Is a strong brown god—sullen, untamed and intractable,
Patient to some degree, at first recognized as a frontier;
Useful, untrustworthy, as a conveyor of commerce;
Then only a problem confronting the builder of bridges.
The problem once solved, the brown god is almost forgotten
By the dwellers in cities—ever, however, implacable,
Keeping his seasons and rages, destroyer, reminder
Of what men choose to forget. Unhonoured, unpropitiated
By worshippers of the machine, but waiting, watching and waiting.

T.S. Eliot

T HE WATERLESS DESERT appears before my eyes, stirring in me a
buried sensation. I am overcome by an intense desire to share
the secret. I dreamt that the river's water dried up and receded to
leave a vast trench, exposing boulders, miscellaneous refuse, and the
skeletons of the drowned. Time as well retreated, and I found myself
a boy in a group of young people. We were exploring the dry riverbed,
making our way between eroded boulders. We collected what the
river had left behind at its bottom: coins, cans, keys, and other items
I do not remember. I also do not remember whether I was tipsy

39

and cannot pin down any other sign of wretchedness or disgust. It was a neutral dream, a non-threatening vision from among the river's many visions. The dream was repeated on successive nights and then disappeared only to pop up years later, resuming its circuit on paths offering many opportunities for reflection and for distant, imaginary travel.

I did not seek an interpretation or attempt to assign a time or place for it. I was, however, confident of one thing: that I was dreaming on behalf of the river, that I was a medium through which the river was dreaming. I was a faithful intermediary for its waters in their resolute flow.

I do not know when this dream began or when it will end. Who remembers a river? Who owns a river? Who restrains a river? Who dares disavow its seasons, phases, or rituals?

The river shuddered and scattered its messages to its naked offspring, the children of the mud, so they could liberate it from captivity. There is no way to keep track of these offspring of the river, for they are the living creatures spread out from its mouth.*

I am not the only dreamer. I am merely a passing dreamer in the aquatic kingdom that great dreamers inhabit. The sage king Utnapishtim was the first and greatest dreamer, who dreamt of the flood. His dream continued and was transported by the river from age to age, from dreamer to dreamer. Then dreams of the river came in succession, and the number of dreamers increased. The river was scattering its messages to those it chose from among the verdant, thick-pelted, fluvial creatures. Thus it chose a wild man of nature

---

* Those whom the river has contacted are many, but among them I remember especially As'ad Muhammad Ali. In his story "The Fisherman and the River," the protagonist dreams of the river itself as a fiery desert. (A)

as the prophet of an epidemic and drought. In my dream, he was a creature with long hair and was preoccupied with oiling the locks of his thick hair with unguent from a jug, which was beset by one rat after another—their muzzles guzzling the oil as it spilled. His spreading dream painted a halo of melancholy yellow light that gave off signs and symbols, dispatching them through the air of future eras. When I received one of his signs, I began to dream of the wild man who had been dreaming for centuries before me. Perhaps he had been present on the bank of the river here in 1831, the year of the great plague, when he began to dream. His dream reached me a hundred and fifty years later. The river hid many dreams in jars, which it deposited in a trough (Buwayb). Sayyab removed them, a jar at a time, experiencing successive visions and pains. The river was the poet's demonic muse, which sucked from his body the nectar of life in exchange for the poetic journeys it disseminated in his dreams.* Thus the poet enjoyed the experience of vast ages, although his lifespan was short. The pains were not on a par with the splendid illuminations that raised the poet to paradises of an imaginary south. Others will go there, to the Eden promised in exchange for their short lives and immense pains. The list of their names is preserved in the Sages' Residence, which is situated at the bottom of the river. No one knows its location; only the river knows.

Once I dreamed that the river was a waterless desert, and that sharp, fiery blades were shearing off the green hair, attempting to encompass it with wires and weapons. When did the dream first occur? I do not remember. But how did it bubble up? A dreamer

---

* See his tribute to the Buwayb River: Badr Shakir al-Sayyab, "Death and the River," in *Badr Shaker Al Sayab: Selected Poems*, trans. Nadia Bishai (Cairo: General Egyptian Book Organization, 2001), 33–36. (T)

from some era came in contact with the river and received from it intimations of that terrible season. Then he shared it with other dreamers. Perhaps the dream occurred in a period before the Iraq-Iran War, many years prior, or only a day before. The dreamers received an intimation of the river's liberation from captivity; or perhaps that was before the war too, for the river's dreams are not in order or dated; they are simply deep. The river precedes its dreams and offers prophecies through its seasons. Then it pushes them into the future. Its flow pushes symbols and then pearly chambers before it, piloting invisible ships. It is a mobile prisoner that welcomes its seasons, breaks its fetters, and guides its ships, overcoming the parameters of its history and choosing for narrators trustworthy, radiant people. It speaks with more than one tongue and exists—vital and gushing—in more than one eye. When it inspired me to narrate for it, I was irradiated with an illumination from Eden: I was dreaming.

Before we were born, our river—the Shatt al-Arab—had no existence, for the two mighty tributaries (the Tigris and the Euphrates) emptied into the basin of the sea at two different locations. At that time our river flowed in the channel of the Tigris. After centuries of separation between the two tributaries, our river was born in some murky way. No historian of antiquity or geographer from the Middle Ages has pinpointed the time. The two tributaries passed through a chain of lakes in the delta of the southern swamps, which were created from the rivers' repeated floods in the sixth century AD. The most important of these were four depressions mentioned by the geographer Ibn Serapion.* They became united as two large lakes: the eastern Tigris lake (al-Huwayza) and the western Euphrates lake (al-Hammar). After the twin tributaries passed through these twin lakes, the Euphrates turned west toward the ancient site of Basra, while the Tigris veered toward the south, parallel to the ancient city of al-Ubulla. The map today shows these two lakes as huge lungs connected to the Shatt al-Arab by two principal canals: the eastern al-Suwayb and the western Karmat Ali.

The two lakes absorbed the waters of the two tributaries for ages, extending their isolated realm, which was established on the rubble of ancient Sumer. Dissolved in this water were the bones of the original inhabitants who had drowned, of their offspring, and of immigrants. When the jet-black night falls over the waters, they resemble a labyrinth. Its canals and reed thickets are home to birds, wild boar, and water buffalo. Slender, tarred boats carry wandering spirits, and there on an undiscovered, small hill (eshan) rising from the waters a divine temple woven from reeds was erected. There Apsu repeatedly poured his sweet water into the vagina of Ti'amat, so that from the cleft of her solid, awe-inspiring thighs the newborn river flowed in a sweet flood that has continued advancing toward the sea and returning in a persistent motion blessed by the full moon for centuries.

The scent of the new birth attracted the distant Euphrates, which died after the destruction of its banks and the obliteration of its flood zones. So it drew close to its twin and joined forces with it for good in a place that was called by many names before finally becoming known as al-Qurna. It slipped beneath the eyes of the troops defending the large forts that the governor of Basra had

---

* Ibn Sarayun, fourth century AH, early ninth century AD. (T)

established where the two rivers met. As for the newborn river, the river gods concealed its name, until the Arab geographers—the great travelers of the Middle Ages—designated it as Tigris of al-Awra' once, the Tigris of Ubulla on another occasion, Shatt al-Basra on a third occasion, and finally Shatt al-Arab ("The Arab Strand"). The final appellation became current after the sixteenth century AD when ships belonging to seafaring merchants from Holland, Portugal, Iran, and England, along with ships from the Ottoman administration, began to navigate it.

The river flows to its inevitable mouth, acquiring from its historic flow topographic knowledge of its banks, the land surrounding it, its tributary rivers, and the sea that embraces it. It has established ethnographic ties with the homes it visits, granting their residents many daily and seasonal gifts. It taught the young people, women, and men the occupations of fishing, agriculture, construction, and pottery. On its banks were planted millions of palm seedlings and fruit trees. The number of date palms increased, and date presses with clattering machinery were established. The relationship began innocently, cautiously, genially, and mysteriously. Then the silence of the gardens developed into a din and into songs. The river became entrenched in the history of the orchards, firms, markets, governments, tribes, merchants, and travelers. It became more densely inhabited and began to show its age, so that sand bars broke through its surface. Dense thickets grew beside it, and animals found habitats in them. Sindbad-type vessels disappeared, as well as the shaded, excursion boats. The singing grew fainter. Anklets, bracelets, basins, and candles disappeared from the stone stairs. The river was isolated by walls guarded with guns. Quarantine posts were established on its sandbars. Upstream, guard barracks, grain elevators, and shipyards were erected. The city grew larger around it, and streets for draft animals and streetcars were built on both sides. Lanterns were hung, and telegraph poles erected. The number of bridges increased. The offices of government agencies and foreign firms towered over it. Prison and hospital, as well as entertainment districts and plants to produce ice and carbonated beverages, were located near its major tributaries. Warships, postal ships, and commercial vessels anchored in its waters. Then terrible seasons for it came in a succession: floods, invasions, and pollution.

One traveler describes witnessing—at the beginning of the twelfth century AD—a lighthouse made of wood and stone. A pulsing green light glittered from its top. The lighthouse was the last landmark on the road to India. When ships approached it, their sailors saw its green light, which appeared to be the river's magical eye. Sediment-ation changed the location of the lighthouse slightly, but it always welcomed new ships and brought them the good news that they had reached fresh water. A sense of security permeated the hearts of the travelers then. Numerous convoys of diverse people passed the light-house. One traveler in particular has stuck in my mind. The pioneer of the Iraqi short story—Mahmud Ahmad al-Sayyid[*]—was standing on the deck of a ship (bajura) leaving for India when his anxious eyes caught sight of the green light of the beacon. He kept his eyes on those regular signals, until his ship disappeared off the maritime horizon. In al-Sayyid's imagination, however, the lighthouse continued beaming pulses of inspiration throughout the nights that the solitary ship was on the high seas. Dr Ali Jawad Tahir thinks it likely that this trip took place during the year 1918–1919, after weeks of unemployment and ennui.[†] I do not know whether al-Sayyid saw

---

[*] Mahmud Ahmad al-Sayyid (1901–37) novelist, short-story writer, and translator. (T)

[†] Ali Jawad al-Tahir, *Mahmud Ahmad al-Sayyid: ra'id al-qissa al-'iraqiya* (Beirut: Dar al-Adab, 1969). (A)

the lighthouse on his return a year later or whether the lighthouse was no longer there, but al-Sayyid wrote *Fi sabil al-zawaj* ("Heading Toward Marriage") after his return from India and published it in 1921. It is the first truly artistic Iraqi short story, although its setting is Bombay. Thirty years later, we saw a similar lighthouse in the middle of the river. We were young and fishing on the rocky shore at night when a flash of throbbing green light suddenly attracted our attention. Then we learned that a small light buoy had been placed over a sunken vessel to caution other ships. It was not big but kept our attention during the following nights. Its pulses guarded the pulsing of our youthful hearts. The lighthouses chronicled the river's years with their slow, methodical pulses: the long life of silent flowing, the changes, upheavals, and promises. These green eyes and hearts gave promise that seasons of terrors would be replaced by spring seasons, date harvests, fishing, riverside weddings, the arrival of ships and of the post, and the intoxication of travel.

Toward the end of the night the river is calm and sends its wise spirit to patrol the city, preceded by its glowing, green eye. Never obstruct a green eye that heads toward you in an alley or knocks on the door of your house. Make way for it and invite it to pass.

The Shatt al-Arab splits the city in two, and its waters flow into hundreds of streams and creeks on both sides. Travelers arriving at the city from the sea would reach it through the Shatt al-Arab, which Mme Delaveau called "The Venice of the Tropics" when she sailed down it in 1881. The natural environment made an immediate impact on the souls of foreigners who encountered the river. What was characterized as "Eastern magic" in the books of the travelers was comprised by the age-old simplicity of the river's life, the isolation of the houses in their gardens, and views of the sun setting over its dense palms. Here, at the hours marking the end of the day, solitude is most pronounced and silence most extensive. Then night brings new fires that shimmer over the tops of the date-filled ships that navigate the river or are moored at the mouths of its tributaries. The Eastern adventure began with an overwhelming sense of the night's stillness. This was inspired by the river, the croaking of the frogs in the thickets on the bank, and fleeting glimpses of lanterns between palm trunks. Meanwhile, hosts at the next port of call concealed unknown pleasures and fears. Morning would sweep them off their feet with the captivating beauty of both banks, as the green current propelled them toward the shade of rows of interlocking palms, pomegranates, bananas, mulberries, and lemon trees, masts and sails, and surprise encounters with Turkish river patrols. Sunset, which crowned the tops of the palm trees with the sun's fiery glow, took away the breath of Lady Dewar, who repeated this tribal Arab saying: "The feet of the palm are in the water; its head is in the fire." That slow descent made other travelers like Niebuhr, Tafranier, Parsons, and Buckingham believe that they were near another Eden; indeed, that they were proceeding down one of the canals of the real Eden. It was difficult for the poverty of the city, the sorry state of its residences, and the emaciation of its inhabitants to erase the initial impact of the river or to deprive them of the ability to discover the world of paradisiacal gardens promised by sacred texts and books of legends.

After a stay of several days, when the travelers—a mixed group of missionaries, merchants, and European adventurers—resolved to leave the city in company with a number of local citizens and officers of the Ottoman government on board a steamship of a local maritime line, they would approach the legendary location where Adam's tree grew. A French ship sank opposite that site with its load of Assyrian antiquities, which had been transported to Basra for reshipment to Paris. The current of the Tigris as it hurried to meet the Euphrates at al-Qurna had snapped the ropes securing the crates of antiquities. These tipped over, the pottery pieces were smashed, and the angry current swallowed them. The anger of the two rivers is absorbed by the Shatt al-Arab in a patient act of consolidation, and their confluence will occasion new delights for the travelers. The sun will set over this place of union, and confronted by this tropical scene they will restrain their gasps in breasts inflamed by the heat and vapors from the river. They will be astonished by the simplicity of half-naked tribal Arabs who hasten to their ship with eggs, chickens, water-melons, and milk, just as they hastened to view the first large steamship to carry the mail when they heard the unfamiliar din of its machinery. These passing Europeans will preserve a special memory of feminine beauty resplendent in the pure brown faces of tattooed Arab women, their noses pierced with silver nose-rings. The river was a route for comfort and punishment, and its waters continued to transport the wares of Asia and India and its post all the way to Europe without interruption. Before the discovery of the route via the Cape of Good Hope, while Basra was linked to India and the world, the British East India and the Lench companies recorded in their ledgers the names of ships and the quantities of their cargoes leaving Basra—dates, rice, cotton, hides, and horses—

and of ships returning with spices, tea, coffee, sugar, tobacco, dyes, wood, iron, lead, medicinal herbs, textiles, ceramics, jewels, and fragrances, together with slaves, dancing women, snake charmers, and turquoise. After the Suez Canal opened, large steamships, laden with emblems of the Western city and its technological innovations, entered Basra. Shortly thereafter came the ships of the British occupation.

In the uncertain climate of the end of 1914, the 16th Cavalry Brigade of Great Britain's Indian Expeditionary Force "D" left its forts on the island of Bahrain, after a rest break during which they took on supplies and an additional number of guides, mercenaries, horses, and mules. Then the Schneider and Manitelli guns defending the Ottoman fort at al-Faw were unable to repulse their advance. The expeditionary forces entered the Shatt al-Arab and proceeded past rows of interlocking palms until they established a base in the Basra basin with all of its facilities for spices, dried fish, apes, whiskey, malaria, grimacing nightmares, and screams of sexual bondage. The expedition advanced toward al-Qurna. There anxiety spread across the faces of the British troops, who were packed together in wooden ships of the type called muhaylat, as their hands clasped their rifles vertically and the river's vapors enshrouded the boats carrying the guns and ammunition. At the confluence of the two principal tributaries the British expeditionary force prepared to ascend the river on the heels of the remnants of the Ottoman forces, following the river's banks in their retreat toward al-Ammara and al-Nasiriya. For a long time these soldiers of the Empire had fallen victim to the curse of twisting Asian rivers, which were lined by forests, where disease, suffocating heat, vermin, scorpions, hostile tribal groups, and the naked howl of death had stalked them. To what unknown would these three murky rivers lead? Spreading plains and the mounds

49

of ancient cities and temples? The tanned faces of silent citizens? What unknown hazards, ambushes, tempests, and contempt for the new conquerors would these sites harbor? Would the river that flowed so serenely return with tales of death and accounts of defeats near the sea? Only the river held the answers.

Basra is a city of many rivers. Historians have counted six hundred major rivers and ten thousand side channels. Al-Baladhuri mentioned the figure of 120,000 rivers. The exact number of these rivers remains the secret knowledge of nature and of the men who dug them (and by whose names they are known) in order to irrigate the fields and orchards granted to them as fiefs by caliphs, princes, and governors. The names of these rivers changed as the names of their proprietors changed and as their huge palaces, which were surrounded by lush gardens, crumbled. The land-tax ledgers and those of the municipality do not reveal the true location of the Ubulla River (the largest of the ancient rivers connecting to the city of Utba ibn Ghazwan) the Abu al-Asad River, which the Caliph al-Mansur's general excavated, the Mubarak River going back to Khalid ibn Yazid al-Qasri, or the other rivers of which traces still turn up on topographic maps based on aerial photography as faint, zigzag lines surrounded by salt marshes.

The remaining waterways that have resisted historic and natural degradation have continued to grant their blessing to the lands, the owners of which have changed repeatedly. These have retained the names of the original excavators to offer evidence of the importance of these green lines for the Arab gardens that shaded the cozy reunions of men like Ma'qil Yassar al-Mazini who dug the Ma'qil Waterway, Marzuq (a 'client' of al-Mansur) who excavated the waterway of Abu Khasib, and Sani' al-Suruj, who linked his name to the Sarrajiya canal.

Search for convivial assemblies beneath grape arbors, palm fronds, and jasmine thickets, for the rustle of silk, the scent of musk, the strains of the lute, the glimmer of bracelets on supple wrists, for giddy looks, plaited roofs, feather fans, silken cushions, nicely appointed skiffs, and family repasts on silk brocade. Search for the orchard that Shahrazad described brilliantly in *The Thousand and One Nights*. Her gracious imagination would not accept anything less than a heavenly orchard where all types of fruit trees, varieties of grapes, colors of flowers, and species of birds intermingled. In this natural shelter hid lovers whose hearts were silent and dissolved in love. The strings of the lute in the hands of the female entertainer interpreted the pain of inescapable separation between two lovers. The vizier's son Ali Nur al-Din had sought refuge with his sweetheart the courtesan Anis al-Jalis in an orchard, while fleeing from the governor's pursuit, before a vessel could transport them to Baghdad. In a similar garden in Dar al-Salam (Baghdad), the lover Nur al-Din relinquished to the caliph his sweetheart the courtesan in return for being received by him. Then Anis al-Jalis sang for the caliph:

> *A young woman whose fingers strummed the lute,*
> *So the soul at this touch began to peek out furtively.*

Before her, the Basran slave-girl Mahbuba sang for the Caliph al-Mutawakkil after Abdallah ibn Tahir presented her to the ruler. The mouths of the sisters of Shahrazad will continue in the future to

repeat the plea made by a character in *The Thousand and One Nights*:
"Buy us fruit, drinks, candied nuts, musk, and five plump hens and
then bring me a lute." Illicit Shahrazad-style assemblies will be
duplicated in dance circles confined to the orchards of Abu al-Khasib,
and the tambourine will move from the slave-girl's hand to the
dancer's, while the voice of Ishaq al-Mawsili will be echoed in that
of Abu Awf.

Search, for you are seeking a stream that the hand of adversity
has not visited. Your skiff, which left the Abbasid orchard, will anchor
at a dam in the Ashar River.

The Ashar is one of the principal rivers of Basra and the artery
of the Shatt al-Arab. It relinquished its palms, walls, and trees to
make way for the street that the governor Sulayman Nazif built in
1909. We can reconstruct daily life at the beginning of the century
from the notes of a customs official, the ledger of a moneychanger,
or the records of foreign consulates. We can similarly collect odd
views of the river from faded photographs recorded by black-box
cameras. We can imagine the flow of traffic at the mule-hire station
located next to the customs office as draft animals laden with
merchandise set off for the city center. Opposite the mule station
was the cargo dock, noisy with workers unloading the ships anchored
there. They were supervised by customs employees and troops—
leaning against the wall—from the Ottoman maritime barracks.
Here in the harbor concluded the sea voyage and days of quarantine,
and then the city's vast cloak would envelop red, yellow, and black
visages of people clad in caps, pants, and hats.

When we first laid eyes on the city, paved roads had been
constructed through the orchards on the south bank, and Ford,
Chevrolet, and Rolls Royce automobiles—along with Philips and

Raleigh bicycles—were circulating along the Shatt al-Arab Corniche. Factories that produced shoes, cigarettes, or carbonated beverages had been established, and the phonograph, fedora, and printing presses had come on the scene. New amusement centers, the cinema, and photography studios had opened. Meanwhile the coffeehouses overlooking the Ashar River had become linked in a chain of wooden-filigree balconies.

The coffeehouses were the first destination for people arriving from distant villages down the Shatt al-Arab, and centers for contact between villagers, merchants, tradesmen, town mayors, tribal chiefs, clerks who drafted petitions, resident aliens, the unemployed, beggars, and smugglers. In these coffeehouses initial agreements were concluded, negotiations were conducted, and the subsequent steps to enter the city's markets and agencies were taken, after hot, sweet sips of tea. The waiter would freshen the tobacco in the water pipes of the men of leisure and the unemployed, and around them other individuals would provide an animated atmosphere for the establishment by engaging in verbal debates, which would become boisterous and mingle with the groans of the machinery of the steam launches thronging the harbor beneath the coffeehouse.

On the other side, the entries of the coffeehouses opened onto a covered passageway separating them from the shops for grains, tobacco, and slippers. People riding or walking along the south bank saw, across the Ashar River, a panorama of the windows of coffeehouses and hotels squeezed in among three bridges. Over the first bridge rose the dome and minaret of the Maqam Ali Mosque. Over the second bridge was a clock erected by an Armenian citizen named Suriyan. The third bridge separated a hotel with many wooden balconies from the Palace of Government. By contrast, the first bridge, which faced some tobacco shops that prepared hand-packed cigarettes, led to the mosque, the grain warehouses, the customs office, the souks for ropes and plaited, palm-frond baskets, and the souk for peddler auctions. The second bridge is opposite a market for shops selling clothing and cosmetics, pharmacies, physicians' clinics, and spice sellers. The third bridge leads to Umm al-Brum Square and al-Ma'qil. The largest coffeehouses leaned against the entrances of the three bridges, whereas the other ones between the bridges began to go out of business. Then all of them were removed when new streets were opened on the north bank and the old wooden bridges were replaced with concrete ones. As the river's commercial activity decreased, it developed into more of a focal point for the city. The ports inside the city were deserted and the boats moved to the banks of the Shatt al-Arab.

The resident of Basra could not escape from the river, for on its banks he built his house with windows overlooking it. He reached it by steps and used it for transportation and washing. Women descended to the river to draw water and to wash clothes and cooking utensils. The city's rivers cut between houses and dispatched side canals so that Basrans could all be its sweethearts and have doorways close to it. The houses' landings were drop-off points for secrets and vows. At the landings, the river deposited its immortal talisman, the talisman of life and death, of spring and birth.

The lady of the house descended to the river early in the morning and found something trapped beneath her house's landing: a chest, a packet of clothes, a dead animal, or a boat. Women met at the landings every morning and evening, and at sunset on special days of the year, you would see them setting out palm nodules laden with lit candles. When the river betrays the trust of these women, it floods, terrorizes, and destroys everything it touches.

The Basran has named his residential neighborhoods after the channels of the Shatt al-Arab, so that neighborhoods like al-Munawi, al-Sarraji, al-Khandaq, Nuhayr al-Layl, Hamdan, and Bab Sulayman have sprung up. These are the names of waterways that still struggle to flow between the ancient houses, orchards, and crumbling banks. Their walls have disintegrated and the surging waters have worn them down. Remnants of bridges survive in the form of wooden posts and the rusty metal rings planted in them. The desperate rivers have grasped the wooden homes constructed on their banks, the curved balconies, the latticework windows, and their changing inhabitants. Then the neighborhoods along the rivers began to disappear. The houses and the decaying balconies have been eliminated. The Romanticism of the bygone shaykhs did not withstand expansion and renewal projects. Residents moved away from the river and built beyond the network of its canals.

Even so the Basrans, children of the rivers, continue to spend some of their time on the quays of their favorite river, the Ashar. The bricks of the vertical bank rise massed together in irregular rows around the openings of the sewer pipes. Plants grow up between the rows of baked bricks and, at the bottom of the bank, on muddy flats where rats multiply. The schools of small fish that swim in the dark sludge coming out of the sewers attract a number of fishermen who cast their lines from the high quay. At night, the lights of the hotels, coffeehouses, and restaurants split asunder its thick shroud and leave calm, glowing traces that do not quiver but collide with

unknown drifting objects. The Basran comes from his new neighborhoods to the ancient river to shop in stores that cling to its banks
and to pause on its bridges that sink under their load.

The river no longer serves the vow-making woman, who has
substituted treated tap water and electric washing machines for its
waters. She has neglected her vows and customs, and the light and
magical images of television have distracted her from participation
in her traditional rites. All the same, the lovesick Basran comes to
stroll in the evening along the riverbank beneath a row of venerable
trees, continuing his walk till he reaches the Shatt al-Arab Corniche,
where he is greeted by waves rippling against the shore and shimmering
at the river's center. Nearby and in the distance, lamps float through
the dark void. A far-off, trembling light approaches, and then the
sound of the motor-launch's engine becomes audible. This is the
miracle of the river, coming after a long estrangement. The sky is
black, and stars glitter in it, surprising the eye, which anxiously
searches for the river's heart. At this time of the night the quays are
deserted, as are the wooden benches along the shores. A speeding
car cuts through the trees' dark shadows, which interlock like strands
of thick hair, and then vanishes down a tunnel through which flows
the sap of ancient tree trunks weakened by the dark wounds of
construction. What is appalling about this continual degradation of
the successive shadows on the road's surface are the hidden tremors,
the spilled spots—like black blood—from the scattered hair of the
unperceived mother, who breathes with a hoarse rustling of her
locks of hair as they dangle in the water, whispering the secret
password that she conveys. For the lover to continue with his walk,
he must know one of these secret words, which he plucks from the
mouth of the venerable, arboreal mother. Another miracle occurs:

the ships that cluster together, sails furled, release the scents of whales, fish oil, dried fish, and fresh, thick bread. With another password the fires of ovens call back and forth to each other from the sterns of the ships, and in the heavy air a sea chantey's plaintive strains quaver. Behind the line of ships a deeper river flows in the Basran lover's heart. From it, ships with lights that glitter on the surface of the deep, silent night depart for distant waters; others rest, sublimely still, waiting for the tides.

Abu al-Khasib
Story Road

He continued to water the palm seedlings' roots;
The seedlings survived but the man died.
Abu Hatim al-Sijistani, *Book of the Date Palm*

I MAGINE WITH ME a man whose job is collecting stories. What road would he take? What would he ride? Who would he be?

I knew a man, the last man my era retained of those who held this profession. They kept busy, moving about and traveling along the Abu al-Khasib road, concealing their inner essence behind familiar external characteristics and common traits. These folks would return from a lengthy trip down its side roads, through its hamlets and bridges, and along its rivers to their lost villages in the orchards beside the road. The storytellers' village was known as the village of Buqay', Hawta al-Tha'alib, Umm al-Ni'aj, Kut Za'ir, Jawkhan al-Yahudi, and by ten other names. Neither dreams nor excursions will help you reach this village more than once in your lifetime, although you may enter it unawares and find yourself face-to-face with a man wearing a white, linen shirt and long pants. He wraps a white kerchief around his head and folds his cloak over his shoulder in exactly the same fashion affected by other story collectors, who place their broad feet in leather sandals, each of which has a strap encircling the big toe. My friend, the last of the story collectors, said that back then he doubted the existence of this village. He suspected that these men with magical tongues had spread out through all the villages and then had vanished inside the heaps of ashes left over from the campfires of barely audible evening sessions along the sides of the road. They had been dispersed by iron pipes, swift wheels, and ocean-going vessels that had swept across the virgin land and rivers, just as castles, forts, and guardhouses advanced against date-drying floors, date-syrup presses, date-packing presses, arcaded streets, river landings, and viaducts. Story-gathering trips came to be limited to dead-end village lanes. So my friend brought back the bicycle he had used on trips and leaned it against the wall of his hut in the depths of the orchards.

By the time I found my way to him, his oldest daughter had moved him into her house in a suburb at the edge of the city, and, as was customary for those in his profession, he had obliterated any path to that nostalgic green spot, protecting it with a chaplet of symbols and deceptive appearances, secretively shielding his eyes with the back of his hand to ward off attacking signals from imaginary stars. At first he himself had doubted the existence of the spot I observed that fall morning in a small village in the district of Uwaysiyan. I had observed there a still pond bordered by dense trees. On its banks was a large, palm-branch seat, which was sheltered by an aged tree's low-hanging branches. The seat was unoccupied and lost in dark shadows, which were reflected in the pond. The story collector said that it was a phantom spot that appeared halfway along the road to the deserted village of the storytellers and that the wasted skeletons of great storytellers had taken turns sitting on the lone chair while leading around intelligent, talking animals.

On that day our friend was on his death bed. His legs and belly were bloated with water, and he had become as heavy as an elephant. His bicycle had been propped in the house's front garden and abandoned there. His demise was attributable to cirrhosis of the liver and dropsy. He was gradually drowning in the liquids that flowed beneath his skin, and his belly had turned into a water-skin that shook with the slightest movement beneath his delicate, slack, smooth skin. Day by day it grew fuller and more inflated, while his head grew smaller and slighter, his jaws hollow, his face lean, and his bones prominent. He was calmly sailing toward his end. He spent the night passing between his bed and the chamber pot. He gazed earnestly at his lap or at the carpets spread beneath his ponderous legs. He attempted to fix his glasses on his bony face. In his dying agony, he objected to having the glasses removed from his face, but over the course of a night and half a day he slowly lost consciousness. When we finally removed his glasses, his pupils were steady, fixed on the flame of the pure waters, the waters of eternity, which began to wash away the roots of the words, the puzzles in anecdotes, and the floating crumbs of stories in a distant stillness. Then he drowned. During the following days the house was silent, the bed empty, and the window left open to the garden with its haggard palm. He had no possessions of any special value, no photo album or expensive set of prayer beads, and no souvenirs of his youth or mementos . . . just a license to pilot a boat, old receipts, and a few clothes in addition to his bicycle, which was abandoned in the garden.

On this bicycle, he had conducted trip after trip, searching for that last, unknown story to collect from tongues constrained by silence and forgetfulness. Paragraph would be united with paragraph, drawn from the most inaccessible places and from the most taciturn people. He would meet his guide—a fox, serpent, or hyena—that would lead him to the end of the road. He was guided to the empty seat on the banks of the still pond, where he heard the same rustling branches—the same rustling previous storytellers had heard from the road—announce his actual arrival and the completion of his journey. With every look, he progressed farther down the dirt road of stillness. Then his bicycle fell between two rows of palm trunks, on a journey of no return. The feeling of having arrived numbed his tongue much as a comparable sensation numbed the storyteller's tongue when he was ready to conclude his narration of a story to a circle of evening revelers gathered around a lamp toward the end of a long night made burdensome by apprehensive waiting once he saw the dust of extinction coat the television screen and the faces around him. This was a greasy dust, which he swallowed with some medicine. I can still remember, after spending evenings in his company, the appearance of his face and wrinkles, which were speck-led with small, dark spots, his glistening lips, the veins of his bent neck, his gnarled fingers, sunken eyes, faint, tremulous voice, white hair, limp ears, the tears trickling down his cheeks, his bent back, heavy steps, bewilderment, thoughts that buzzed past each other like flies, and his dispassionate wait for his final journey. The story collector mounted his bicycle in response to a delicate summons from his animal familiar, which assumed the shape of a bell, a flower, a succulent singing mouth, a convoy of ants, a fissure in the earth, a stray feather, or a spider dancing on its thread. He said, "Observe what you see carefully. Fix it in your memory and don't forget it. Follow the rays of light spilling across the asphalt, over the water, and under the bridges." That was his counsel before his shadow vanished. He whispered, "Stroke the void, drink silence, and breathe to your last gasp. Then close your eyes and allow things to settle into the furrows of your memory. Express it as though you were seeing it for the first time. Disseminate it, allow it to slumber, and do not attempt to cross-examine it. It will sprout, bloom, diffuse its perfume, and utter its statement. The story will come to you and unfold like a mute flower. Open your hands to its unfurling leaves as they gleam in the dawn's first light. The crimson letters will try to make your flesh speak and penetrate your heart and mind to provide an antidote to your sorrows and insomnia." His counsel resembled an incantation, a sweet tidbit, or even a sting that heals with its cauterizing pleasure. It reached me beside the twisting road of stories. The story collector bequeathed me his bicycle in appreciation of my care for him. So I rolled out the old bicycle, which lacked brakes and accessories, and surprised the mourners who were leaving the house.

At noon one summer day, I headed south on the bicycle. Its wheels were slow on the hot asphalt but then soared down the breezy route through the orchards. A melancholy rustling I could not identify stirred between the trees. It sounded like sighs and heavy breathing fused together in the shade. I descended into an orchard with pale vegetative life and small gray birds. Fleeting specters climbed the palm trees, disappeared among fronds, or were swallowed by lurking brooks. I rocked back and forth on a thin thread of wakefulness stretched between mulberry trees, pomegranates, bananas, and grapes, between the scent of the earth and the fragrance of forgotten, feral flowers, beneath setting suns and flying mirrors. Broad leaves stroked my face and thorns stuck to my skin and clothes. As I walked into an unexpected but delightful little dell, a grassy carpet of red flowers closed around my face, locking out the day's light. From tiny windows between the fronds, the features of a radiant, childish face appeared, bowing and smiling. Then it began to whisper, singing at times and making sly confessions. The embrace was larger than the grassy dell itself and gradually faded away. The stillness evolved into birds that passed overhead and then melted away in the spreading brilliance of lofty and luminous apertures. Heat streamed from fissures in the earth, and there came a shout from the riverbank. It was a wild, dry voice that did not reach even as far as the opposite bank. In fact, swift, opposing energies and currents and white paws rising from distant, shady thickets captured the sound. This was not a river, an orchard, a bed, or a tomb. This was not a day, air, light, and shade. This was not insects and butterflies. This was not fragrance, wings, or thorns. This was not a dream. What was it then? Do I know? Did I fall asleep beneath a pomegranate tree ablaze with red, flowery goblets dangling like bells swaying in the mysterious, teasing breeze with a plaintive moan or drink from a pottery cup, the shifallah tree's dark red blossoms' nectar presented by the hands of enchanted maidens during a picnic lunch on the orchard's tall grass?

During my following trips, I gradually strayed farther from the beginning of the road, by a bridge leading to the city. It is the first in a series of many bridges. The bridges are not the only features of the road and its stages; there are also the aged trees on both sides, the hedges of its orchard, its huts and coffeehouses, the entries to the lanes of its villages, its buildings, mosques, and many curves. I rested on the huge trunk of a tree that had been severed from its stump and dumped by the side of the road. From the story collector I heard a tale about these logs. The tree had stood at the entry of a side lane, which led to a village, and served as a resting spot for people leaving the village or traveling along the roadside. One day the story collector encountered a young man there who was an expert chess player. The youth spread a piece of cloth over the level top of the tree's stump and removed chess pieces from a bag he carried inside his garment. The pieces, which were carved from roots, had amazing shapes. The young man lined them up on the chessboard as though setting out something precious. The story collector watched as the youth moved the pieces. He won all the chess matches with a number of carefully considered moves that demonstrated an extraordinary skill. When asked his name, the young man said, "Abdullah." This name, though, was merely a legendary invention that seemed suitable for the royal game. He spoke in a voice other than that of the young chess player through whom news of bygone times was transmitted. A chess master was playing from inside his clothing. The story collector imagined that his opponent was the prince of Granada Abdu Ilah al-Zaghal, who was imprisoned by his brother the ruler in a castle overlooking Malaga. There he competed with chess masters whom he chose with his brother's consent. At the same time he received from them news of battles raging around the last strongholds of Andalusia from the diagrams the chess masters superimposed on the game board to make it represent the battlefield. Thus the imprisoned prince guided the cavalry of Andalusian army or strengthened positions vis-à-vis his Castilian foe Ferdinand V and his wife Isabella, the Queen of Aragon.* The story collector learned new opening moves and heard strange tales from the youth, but his attempts to find him again proved futile, for he vanished and never appeared at the fallen tree trunk after that precious day.

One day I reached a huge sidr tree mentioned in a story by the previous storyteller and found a clay water jar standing on the wooden winch. Around the jug were the ashes of campfires and the remnants

---

* Werner Bergengruen (AD 1892–1964) wrote a short story ("The Royal Game") about the imprisoned prince. Abu Abdullah al-Zaghal, who ruled from AH 888 to 892, was one of the kings of Granada. (A)

from travelers' chance encounters. The pot had no known owner who might continue filling it, and wayfarers who chanced to meet at that spot did not wonder why it was there. They would trade news, tobacco, and stories. Some would barter goods, settle debts, or conclude a new contract before separating. I heard from my twin a choice anecdote about one of the people from the road's villages. He was leading his cow to market in the city and, when he reached the sidr tree, decided to rest beneath it till the sun was no longer directly overhead. The villager tied his cow to the tree trunk. While he slept, the cow circled the tree to face the direction from which they had come. When the man awoke from his nap, he unfastened the rope and set off with the cow toward his house, in the opposite direction from the market, for he had taken his bearings from the location of the intelligent cow. You hear this anecdote and others like it and then rise to drink from the jug. So you remove the cover from the water, which is flooded by the abundant shade. Because the faces of nocturnal visitors have so frequently bent over the jar's still surface, their dry, wrinkled, thirsty features have settled on its conical bottom. Leaning over the jug's broad, round opening, like them I discovered the wrinkles of my face, and my gaze sank to its imaginary bottom. Green slime coated it inside and out. My face collided with the invigorating coolness. Then my gaze discerned other submerged items at the bottom: spadix segments, prayer beads, worms, pebbles, tiny leaves from the tree, assorted teeth, and particles of daylight filtered by the tree's leaves. Attached to the lid was a chain for the jug's cup, but the cup was gone. I searched around for the lost cup and then leaned over the clear surface, apprehensively closing my eyes, until my lips reached the cold surface. So I sipped the water.

Repeated trips lifted the curtain from other scenes, but their formless elements changed with variations in the heat and shade before they could be named. Name them if you can, but you will fail unless you rest repeatedly beneath the pomegranate tree at noon in that summer orchard and drink from the cups of the shifallah trees. Another person will be born within you: a storyteller who directs his bicycle down the imaginary road and overtakes the scions of silver-tongued storytellers.

The 1950s were splendid years, not because those years saw the demise of feudalism, parliamentary elections, the flowering of printing and journalism, and Khudayri Abu Aziz's broadcast parties, and not because they were novel years for automobiles, movies, the circus, art exhibitions, bicycle races, and soccer tournaments. For no clear reason, the city appeared splendid to the eyes of students arriving from nearby rural areas as they discovered new roads for their scrawny feet and penetrated ever farther down its unknown paths.

At the beginning of the fifties, I transferred into the middle-school section of the centralized secondary school and entered its vast art room on the second floor. It was a large studio with thick walls and tall windows, which provided a first sanctuary for a voyage of discovery and for daydreams. Our art teacher was tall, thin, and stern-looking. His awe-inspiring influence penetrated his fingers, which made silent dirt speak and pursued vanishing horizons in village paintings, some of which he hung on the walls of the studio alongside paintings by previous teachers and gifted students who had passed through this studio before us. On that day, nature was silent and so were rural retreats, faces of domestic life, and scenes of urban misery, which were the dominant subjects of the paintings hung on the walls of the studio in the 1950s. Delicate innocence and childish sensitivity—at the hand of our teacher—fluctuated between shadow and light, like a solitary sail buffeted by a storm at sea. The painting *The Torn Sail* and a second canvas featuring a pottery vessel, a lemon, and a dull knife were the vanguard of a dark vision that led the student artist to his slow death of pulmonary tuberculosis. Similarly, paintings—inspired by an English Romantic artist—of homeless children, a nursing mother, dock workers, the guide carrying a blind man on his back, and other such paintings drenched in dark brown and vivid yellow exhausted the compassionate impulse of our trembling fingers on rainy winter mornings. Pictures were stacked against the walls of the studio. They left for the annual school exhibitions and then returned. Holiday dust coated them, as well as the clamor of demonstrations, and severe weather ravaged them. Once we graduated, the streets of the city snatched us for its willing sacrificial offerings and prepared for us solitary places, promenades, and scattered corners, which we compared to the solitude of our studio, because our solitary retreat was smaller than one of its warm corners. Every faint line a pencil drew on the easel generated the direction of lines of our subsequent coal-black days. Each face, body, breast, hand, pot, vase, hearth, glass, oven, slaughterhouse, train, prison, creek, tree, bridge, steamship, sensation, impression, hope, and rebellion that we portrayed in our original pictures came to life later and confronted us like a preordained prophecy. What has not yet put in an appearance is lying in wait for us around a future corner. Our studio was a cave of surprises and prophecies that will accompany us to the grave or the throne of tragedies on the boulder of Prometheus. Thus the time has come to talk about a unique painting that appeared on the studio wall one morning. I saw no fewer than three copies of it in school exhibitions of the 1950s. The studio copy was a response to Muhammad Radi's original painting, which was exhibited in a group show back then. There were not many details in the painting. It was nature raw: a dull-colored pit on the Abu al-Khasib road. Included in it were fleeting echoes of the age and its scattered lines, which formed part of the road, part of a short, empty space. It was permeated by a desolation derived from Munch's characteristic style. In the picture, the road veers off between two rows of palm trees and then disappears around an abrupt curve. The road slants down in a dwindling funnel shape at the heart of the painting—or the heart of nothingness—where there is a gate to nowhere or a vortex of loss. That distance, which appears to be longer than the road with all its twists and curves, suggests an endless journey and a spiraling place that draws its dreaming victims to their unknown destiny. Something fell into the depths and the stillness swallowed it . . . a vehicle, a bicycle, a man, or the painter himself who vanished behind the imaginary portal of palm trees. Absence and presence balance each other in the life of travelers on the road. The very same feeling afflicted me when I was gazing at a similar strip of the road during one of my youthful bicycle trips. A section of the road appeared before me as it would have appeared to any other traveler or to a contestant in one of the bicycle races held in those distant days. Here is the story for you.

When we were young—pupils in elementary school—our greatest, giddiest hope was to possess a bicycle. There were many bicycles in those days, and the most famous advertisement for the Philips bicycle showed an African boy on a speeding bicycle as a lion pursued him. Every shop that rented bicycles had at least one copy of this poster, which overflowed with force, magic, and speed. Yes, bicycles and horse-drawn carts were the most famous landmarks of the bygone years. Bicycle races were always being held, supervised by some top official. They would normally begin in a remote rural village and end somewhere in the city. The responsible official would sit for long hours waiting for the arrival of the last mud-spattered bicycle or for it to be brought back in a truck because it was unable to move or operate. Most of the contestants rode ordinary bicycles like a Raleigh, Rudge, or Philips. A few had special racing bikes. Naturally we had champions who could traverse lengthy distances over unpaved and unmarked roads or perform acrobatic stunts on their bicycles to dazzle the crowds standing on the sidewalk. Our city's champion was a cyclist known to men, women, and children alike. Because he was both an exhibitionist and a swift racer, he was recognized by both city-dwellers and rural folk when he shot down their roads like an arrow. In addition to that, his favorite and thrilling sport, when there was no road race, was to ride a high unicycle, teetering and staying upright on it only with difficulty as he roamed the city's streets, trailed by delighted and admiring children. For the long races, people would crowd both sides of the course, yelling to the rider leading the pack that he was our hero, regardless of who it was. Our champion continued to be viewed with admiration and curiosity for a long time. After that he bought a modern automobile, gave up riding bicycles, and joined an athletic association that frequented the athletes' coffeehouse.

Back when our story took place, the athletic coffeehouse attracted swimmers, wrestlers, and runners whose championship days were behind them. Just when we were ready to forget the cyclist, he was dreaming of another race with which he would end his athletic career, which was brimming with marvels. Two swift wheels turned incessantly in his head. After we became convinced that he had abandoned the solitary life that cyclists prefer and that his hands were scrubbed clean of oil, he sold his strange unicycle with the raised seat. The former champion had decided to participate in a masters' competition of club representatives. He chose a bicycle from a friend's shop, greased it, and tightened its wheels. Then he placed it on the road in a long course with a large number of former champions eager for one last adventure. Trucks carried the competitors to the starting line. Noticing the tepid looks of people turning away from him, the former champion felt depression and sorrow pass like a frightening cloud over his professional resolve. This cloud did not lift. It accompanied him all the way to the murky end, an end that is always reported in a different way in the athletes' coffeehouse.

The race began from the farthest point of the Abu al-Khasib road and was supposed to end at the entrance to the large garden on the Shatt al-Arab Corniche. The first stage of the race was along a straight, open road. Nothing happened to diminish our champion's certainty that he would win. The second stage, containing thirty bridges, had many curves and was shaded by closely planted date palms. It seemed a road that stretched on endlessly. What happened during this stage can be explained only by one inference. The silence of a summer afternoon, the fragrance of the flowers and trees behind the road's hedges, the sun's beams falling on the level asphalt from gaps between palm fronds, and the road's surprise turns must have caused the two wheels in the champion's head to turn with astounding speed. So he gained a substantial lead over the other competitors before he perceived that he was all alone and had lost the course. He entered a side lane through the orchards, one of those lanes that are little traveled and that most often lead into a mirage. A long time had elapsed since another cyclist passed on the public road. Once again the wheels in his head began to turn. Their speed was accelerated by the tedious solitude among the palm trees, the warm breath of the plants and trees, and the total absence of any scent of a human being. He felt he could soar above the palm fronds and then descend over the top of a small wooden bridge to a grassy depression. He entered a gate crowned by grapevines to begin a road no competitor had ever taken.

At the finish line, the prizes had been distributed, the government and athletic officials in charge of the race had left, the crowd waiting for the racers had dispersed, and the truck that had picked up racers who had collapsed or whose bicycles had broken down had arrived. Evening came and the lights on the poles hidden among the trees of the Corniche were turned on. Meanwhile, vendors were collecting the soft-drink bottles that had been thrown beneath the trees. The dancing shadows around the finish line, which was marked on the asphalt, pushed against a woman and two children crouched there in a huddle, waiting for the professional racer, whose bicycle had not arrived. Nor did it arrive in the coming days.

A small search party set out the next morning. They combed the sides of the public road the race had used and questioned farmers and their children. No one, however, had witnessed the speeding bicycle as its wheels sank beneath the trellised gate on the road of no return. That gate resembled the deep, funnel-shaped trough in the painting in the studio. Behind the gate, the curving, spiraling athletic route began, with a magnetic verdure, devoid of any sound. The airborne bicycle was drawn into its eternal orbit, as the competitive racer on his bicycle circled nearly identical paths that kept branching off beneath the shade of thick palms. There, two feet pump up and down with a mechanical rhythm. His head is bent over the handlebars, and the bicycle advances at a steady, constant speed. When we remember this story, ancient perfumes overwhelm us with promises and secrets. We recall the widow who stayed for a long time beside the white finish line, as vehicles' wheels and the ghostly shadows of the aged trees swept past her. The events in this story could happen to any of us—no question about it—we who are the sons of the imaginary road.

André Gide tells us about a mosque in Tunis. When he entered, he found its courtyard to be clean, calm, and radiant with sunlight. Shadows and the scent of prayer vigils lurked in its chambers. Then the mosque's tranquility penetrated his inner being, which was troubled by errant, libidinous concerns. Mosques had a similar effect when they were encountered by Flaubert, Gérard de Nerval, Rimbaud, Camus, Genet, and Garaudy in various different Islamic countries—as did the rural roads, which are saturated with the greenness, sunshine, and solitude of the rural regions. This would be as if I—on seeing a British general stop a convoy of trucks transporting his soldiers or a European tourist bound to his brown guide— offered both of them refuge from Basra's midday heat in one of the roadside mosques beyond al-Sarraji mosque. These are hidden among date palms, between one bridge and the next, one bend and the next, and one farm plot and the next. The general or the tourist would enter—through a low portal—a courtyard paved with square bricks, which have been freshly washed, and seek the shade of the mosque's still, tidy portico, the shade and silence of which are increased by a short minaret, the masonry dome, a lone date palm, jugs of water lined up for ritual ablutions, and a pair of tame birds. Strangers off the street, in different eras, have noticed a man napping in the portico. His rough feet protrude from beneath his garment, and his sandals along with his knapsack are propped beside him. He is asleep, and no one knows when he fell asleep, when he will awake, or what is in his knapsack. Perhaps the strangers will enter the oratory and explore the rooms of the mosque, the doors of which are ajar. Then they pause before a locked room. Its ancient wooden door with its bronze handle and the water jug are shaded by the palm tree. The passersby notice a man sleeping in the shade of the porticos of subsequent mosques, and a locked room in addition to all the open ones.

After the visitors have left, when darkness settles and the night grows still, the man rises from his slumbers, opens the door of the locked room, and lights the lamp. Then he leans over his papers, copying another manuscript from the original texts that are piled on the book boxes stacked in the room. In all the remaining, similar mosques hidden among palm trees, there are also copyists. Their number, the day they appeared or disappeared with their manuscripts, and their sponsor are all unknown. The most that can be pinned down are the dates of the copying, as recorded at the end of the manuscripts, and the layers of soot that have accumulated in the lamp's niche. The locked room—in any of the mosques along the road— if you happen upon it, may have been the room of Abu Hatim al-Sijistani and twenty of his pupils and apprentice Qur'an-reciters, who kept increasing in number after his death. It would then have contained many of his books, including thirty-seven that bibliographers consider lost and a number of other books that Ibn Nadim listed in his *Fihrist* and that book collectors and editors have sought for centuries. Another lucky scholar discovered a manuscript of the book *Kitab al-nakhla* ("Book of the Date Palm") by Abu Hatim, open to its final page. The scribe Muhammad ibn Hakam ibn Sa'id had finished the final line of it, including the date of its completion as Sunday with two nights remaining from the month of Jumada II of the year AH 394.* We do not know how this sole surviving copy was carried to Agrigento and to the hands of the Italian Orientalist Bartolomeo Lagumina, who published it in Palermo, Sicily, in AD 1873 with a commentary in Italian. Our consolation, that of those of us who travel the road, comes in a new, revised edition published by Dr Hatim Salih al-Damin in 1985 with ample commentaries and a useful introduction.

Would Abu Hatim permit us to add another line to it? I think not. His penetrating eyes and the eyes of his student copyist as well as tracks of lizards that had walked in date syrup became part of the many commentaries in the manuscript's margin, and other indications and punctuation marks look out at us from the new copy, like a heavy cluster of dates ready for harvest. When we search for a pursuit as productive as reading a rare manuscript, we think of planting a palm seedling. A burning desire to finish a book punctually is often extinguished only by the obligation to plant a palm seedling before the final call reaches us. About this meritorious deed, Abu Hatim relates a story in his *Kitab al-nakhla*:

> Al-Harith ibn Dakkin related that Ibn al-Khattab said, "If I heard the call while holding a palm seedling, I would attempt to plant it before the call reached me." †

---

* Abu Hatim Sahl ibn Muhammad ibn Uthman al-Sijistani, *Kitab al-nakhla*, Hatim Salih al-Damin, ed. (Beirut: Dar al-Basha'ira al-Islamiya, 2002), 21–22. (T)

† Ibid., 52. The shout or call suggests Judgment Day. (T)

Abu Hatim traces the stages of development of the seed till it becomes a seedling and describes the stages of development of the seedling until it matures into a date palm. He pursues the fruit's relative ripeness from being unripe, to ripe, to dry, and then syrupy. So the first step for the date pit is the planting. The date palm sprouts from a cavity in its back. Then it breaks forth and becomes visible, becoming a sheath and then the sheath a palm leaf. It branches from this stalk to become three. When the stalks multiply and subdivide into branches and its stem is rooted in the dirt, it becomes a palm seedling. Then we learn whether it is male or female. Next the seedling escapes from hands that reach for its crown. Following this, it is a palm tree that is neither short nor tall and begins to bear date clusters. After Abu Hatim enumerated the stages of development of the palm seedling, whether it emerged from a date pit or was a sucker cut from the mother palm's trunk, he gave for the whole date palm ninety descriptions that correspond to its changing forms. Once the sucker has been cut from it, the cloned palm tree is called the mubtil. This term was borrowed for houses, since a batil house can stand alone as a detached house, separate from other houses. A female virgin is called batul, and a monk is called mubattil. After some lines of admonition, we learn how the palm tree shares descriptive terms with the rest of creation. The juvenile date palm increases in height until it is stripped of the sheaths of its leaves, when it is described as al-qirwah, al-sahuq, and al-taruq. When it becomes quite tall, it is called muhjira, and hoopoes build nests in the crown. Finally the stem of the palm grows frail, its crown diminishes, its leaves decrease in number, and its head leans to one side. This then is the end of its life and the beginning of its death, the start of the final journey of sap through its veins. It is an end that vexes the farmer in the south and that lodges in the dreams of the poet like the rotting columns of peasants' houses. How many a young palm has had a river eat away at its roots until they dry out and turn into wood for women feeding ovens and hearths, a bridge for people to cross streams, a support for water pails, or roof posts.

Among the metaphors for date palms are phrases that refer to beauty or ugliness, power or weakness, straightness or bending, fertility or barrenness, succulence or dryness, and other such conditions of the seed and seedling as they grow and bear fruit. This continuing experience resembles that of man as he lives or creates. We can infer from the resemblance between the date pit and the female genitalia that there is a fundamental tie, since they are both essential to the continuation of the species and to its homogeneity. Between the palm tree and animals like camels and sheep or men and women there is a resemblance both in their changing or accidental characteristics and in their inherent attributes. In this relationship, the palm tree should be considered the original, and the others derivative. The date palm and the others appear to have commenced from a single nature, from the center of which sprouted the palm's lofty trunk that spread its shadow over nature's expanse. This is what an isolated desert oasis shows you when camels gather in the shade of its palm trees and rub against their trunks. Consider too a trail with palms lined up along it like the lines of words on the page of a book.

"Basra is the land of the date palm," said Abd al-Rahman ibn Abi Bakra as he planted the first palm seedling in the sands of the military camp city. From Basra the gardener Akbuba carried palm seedlings to Baghdad and planted them around his house on the Karkhaya River. Similarly, the Burhi date palm was transported from the orchard of the Zaydan family in Abu al-Khasib to Iraq's plantations.* Before these men, there were date palms growing in Iraq's fertile lowlands in virgin groves that spread, thanks to the hands of unknown farmers who were residents of the Tigris and Euphrates delta. They traveled there from the south of the Arabian Peninsula with bags of dates and date pits. When Khalid ibn Safwan set forth with a Basran delegation heading for Syria, he described this unknown land to Caliph Abd al-Malik ibn Marwan as follows: "Our houses are golden, and our river is a marvel. The beginning of it is dates, the middle is grapes, and the end is qasab reeds."

When we look at the map drawn by Yusuf Nasir al-Ali for Basra during the first four Muslim centuries, we see he noted the location on it for twenty-two markets and their specialties. These spread between al-Kala' (the river port) and al-Mirbad (the external market along the desert).† The noisiest and largest of these markets stretched along the two sides of the Fayd River that branched off from the Shatt al-Arab, around the bridge of the Bilal River, which connects the Fayd River with the Ma'qil River, and around al-Rizq city and its gates. We overtake a caravan arriving from the desert on the Mirbad Road, which traverses Basra from west to east, passing by the slave market, which is opposite the portal of the "Friday" mosque in the center of the city. The caravan sells some of its wares in markets along the road and buys supplies: flour, meat, and wine. Resuming its journey, it reaches the Bilal Bridge and presents to the bridge's muhtasib and his workers a tenth as payment of the duty.

---

* Abd al-Qadir Bash A'yan, *al-Nakhla*. (A)

† For the markets of Basra, see Yusuf Nasir al-Ali in *al-Khalij al-'arabi*, 1973, no. 1. (A)

Then it sets down its bags at the gates of al-Rizq city, opposite the large markets of al-Kala'. The caravan remains for days while ships arriving from the sea by the Ubulla River unload their goods in the caravansaries of the port. Then they return with dates, perfumes, and textiles. The quays of the harbor are noisy with the clamor of porters (South Asian Jats, Asawira, Siyabaja, and Arabs), Indian sailors, Basran merchants, vendors of palm seedlings, dates, discount dates, palm trunks, palm fronds, and palm mats. Among all these we recognize the teachers from Qur'an schools, money changers, tariff collectors, and a mixed group of slave traders, thieves, beggars, and masters of various other professions. It is date season, which al-Jahiz called the days of saram. The harbor was full of ships unloading and departing daily with dates, and the chits of the money-changers passed from hand to hand.

This season, which was noisy with the world's languages and the ringing of gold dinars and foreign coins, when marvelous clothing and ships were seen, was repeated each year even after the city abandoned its desert location following its total destruction in the first year of the seventh century AH and moved closer to the dense groves of date palms along the Shatt al-Arab. Back then, merchants circulated among themselves qurush, Ottoman liras, fictive shamis,* Persian tomans, and pounds sterling, which took the place of the last coin from Abu Bakra's currency. It had fallen from a hole in a sack fastened to the waistband of a farmer returning to his hut among the date palms. The sands of invasions then covered it and it was trampled deeper into the dirt by the feet of policemen and landowners and the hooves of horses until an employee in an English trading company discovered it and used it as an emblem to stamp on crates packed with Basra dates before these

---

* The shami was an obsolete or fictive currency that was used in the nineteenth century by Basra's merchants to value the dates they traded. (A)

were transported from local presses to the firm's steamships, which departed for the markets of Europe, America, and Asia with the slogan, "Best Dates in the World."

Appraising dates, trimming date palms, and harvesting dates were three operations that since ancient times had been carried out by appraisers, sharecroppers, trimmers (pickers), harvesters (gleaners), and processors. One harvest season after another drew numerous caravans of date pickers, and presses and markets were set up in the shade of the palm fronds or by the light of campfires and lanterns. The harvest festivals lasted from August to October across an area of 150,000 jirib* until the Dog Star announced that all the various different types of palm-leaf date baskets (jilal, khasasif, and qawasir) were filled, and that the dates were heaped up on the drying floors, and that the long strip extending for more than a hundred miles near the Shatt al-Arab was empty of migrant farm workers.

In an out-of-the-way plot on the edge of this humid, green strip, I heard a tale about the watchman for a yukhan.† It was related by the skipper of a ship that transported dates from Basra to ports along the Arab Gulf.

Anyone who follows a returning sailboat, like the one that inspired this story, after it has unloaded its dates in the emirate of Umm al-Qaywayn will fall into a fever like that inspired by a yearning for the horizons. He will see the ship suspended on a mud bank at the outlet of the Shatt al-Arab as the sunset gripped its mast and darkness cast its thick cloak over the three sailors. The words will reverberate in the river air, and their slow harmonies will settle into spaces along

---

* A *jirib* is equivalent to 3.967 meters. (A)
† Yukhan or jukhan: a drying floor for dates and by extension a date grove. Residents of Abu al-Khasib pronounce "j" as "y." (A)

the muddy shore. The eyes of the men on board were attracted to a faint light beyond the riverbank and behind the trunks of a row of date palms. The two sailors obeyed their captain and descended to a small dinghy to search for food in the nearby orchard. The night passed and morning appeared as the sun topped the palm trees' crowns without the return of the two envoys. Next we will hear the story from the third man, the skipper waiting on board the stranded ship. The rising water raised the ship, and then the experienced skipper was able to guide it to a haven on the opposite shore. He returned in a dinghy the following morning to search for his two companions, conjecturing that these two men had been carried some distance along the river and had moored their dinghy below the hut in which the watchman for the yukhan lived. This was one of those shacks scattered through the river's date groves. That night the hut's lamp emitted the gleam of a forgotten life behind the hedge of thorny trees. The two men would have tied the dinghy to a tree, climbed up the bank by a ladder composed of smooth palm trunks, and approached the door of the hut. After rowing half the day, the skipper reached the same hut at the door of which all traces of the two sailors had vanished some nights before. Instead of a ladder of smooth palm trunks, the skipper discovered steps of porous, black stone and a towering, massive tree that showered the river with cottony yellow flowers. He was even more amazed by the extensive gap, like a deep mouth, which gargled green water before swallowing it, in the base of the tree. The hut was empty except for a mat, a water container, a thick stick the absent watchman used to bolt the hut's door from the inside, and a hanging lantern. The skipper went out to the vast yukhan and toured its widely spaced, tall, skinny, feeble date palms. Throughout the grove he observed dates scattered in piles covered with matting.

The dates were dark and had seen a succession of years and seasons, while the rains had washed them for years. At the edge of the yukhan, the skipper came upon a date-syrup press that showed traces of old syrup in its uncovered channel. A glance around the date-syrup press showed the yukhan to be an abandoned site no foot had trod since the end of a bygone summer when the scorching south wind had dried out its shade and then swept it into the rivers.

The skipper returned to the hut and leaned against a wooden column in front as evening spread like a coarse, fibrous cover. Had he come to the wrong hut just as his two comrades had? Or had their footsteps ended at this yukhan as had those of previous lost men looking for assistance? At the beginning of this rough evening he had a special sense of the riddles created by times of solitude— like viewing the expanse of the sea, long nights spent waiting in ports, and the pursuit of fugitive horizons. This empty hut resembled those, and, should a person emerge from any of these, he would open the door to a second riddle. With repetitions and movement like this, a man lives more years than his lifespan and advances into gray periods. The skipper was pondering this new riddle when he sensed a thin shadow approaching him. Then the yukhan's aged watchman passed and walked slowly into the hut. After a time lantern light emerged from the hut. Put simply, the watchman was blind. This is what the skipper assumed when the watchman came so close to him that he almost bumped the skipper. He became convinced that he was right as he examined the face of the man, who was lying on the mat. It was a taut, wizened face, and the two eyes were like those of one of Luqman ibn Ad's seven eagles.

The rest of the tale became confused in the skipper's telling, or perhaps I have forgotten how it ended. The tired watchman either sank into an eternal slumber the moment he lay down—or the skipper discovered in the abandoned yukhan the remains of the watchman, who had been sleeping in the hut for an extremely long time and who had turned into a cadaver with blue bones. The skipper returned to his ship and three years later met his two companions, who told him they had been guests of the yukhan's watchman on the night in question, in a place they did not remember very well, and that they had returned the following morning to find that the ship was no longer stuck in the mud. They said that the watchman actually was a slave who had fled with a small contingent of the Zanj after the battle of al-Mukhtara. Then a land owner had picked him up and made him a watchman for his grove. After the sickle of the fates had harvested the landowner in some bygone era, the watchman had remained in his remote hut, outliving his master by many decades.

In the past I have told some stories, but all my tales taken together do not rival a single one in the bag the story collector carried through the villages and expansive districts of the south. This man appeared as an itinerant salesman or a hawker trading in scrap metal and was observed sleeping in a corner of a mosque in Yusufan. He surprised others by wading into the Akhras River, by peering out of a crevice in a wall in Muhayjaran or near the tomb of Abbas ibn Mirdas al-Salmi on the Qawus River in al-Baljaniya, or by fishing in the A'waj River in al-Khawaz District. He was a musician at a springtime celebration around the tomb of Abu al-Hamd, a sailor on a ship laden with licorice in one of the twelve rivers of al-Dawasir District, a farmer in the extreme south in the orchards of the Ma'tuq River, or perhaps he was a thief or a highwayman in the night's passes or on the outskirts of cemeteries, a cobbler making yellow leather boots, a grave digger, a blacksmith, or a seller of rope twisted from palm fibers in the Abu al-Khasib market. Whether he carried a knife-sharpening wheel, a machine for mending Chinese porcelain, or an instrument for carding cotton, or was steering a dusty bicycle weighed down with bottles of a herbal tonic,* his unforgettable features were recognized by villagers and travelers alike. When he disappeared from their villages and no longer hawked wares down their lanes, they predicted an end to the happy age of tales.

You will search for him in vain beneath Barham's tree by the jug that still awaits visitors in the tree's shade. Here or there you will listen to some information or an anecdote taken from his reports, stories, and witty remarks, but no one will be able to guide you to him. Thus you will only encounter him in some chance assembly by the road, although there will be nothing about his appearance to distinguish him from any other wayfarer. An old crone told me that this storytelling man was a demon that had assumed human shape. Then I was immediately reminded of the yukhan's watchman with the attractive spider-like appearance that commanded the attention of ears and souls. I would surely trade my pen and my imagination for a sack of his stories; but how impossible! The age of Mephistopheles and Tantalus has departed; compassionate demons no longer exist.

---

* Al-Miya al-saba'a: a medicinal brew. (A)

Al-Zubayr
The Camel's Eye

Bending over the sand,
She searches for a ring.
Wanting prickly pear, she eats colocynth.
Wailing or panting,
Her camel froths at the mouth,
And the wind howls.

Husayn Abd al-Latif

ZZZZZZZ . . . THE WINDS roll this Thamudi consonant and toss it down on the northern border of the desert elevation of the Arabian Peninsula. The sands' roar puts the extra dot on the middle consonant in Arabic to distinguish between *kathaba* (assemble) and *kataba* (write). The one additional dot that distinguishes "t" from "th" in the Arabic script rises like a grave. A camel's hoof traces the name "Zubayr" where his tomb lies. Consider these words with the same consonants as his name: *zabara* is a synonym for *kataba* (write), *al-zabr* for *al-kitaba* (writing), and *al-zabur* for *al-kitab* (book). The city is built on the grooves of the word with mud-brick houses that cling together, narrow twisting streets, and open spaces for the mosque, souk, governmental agencies, walls, wells, and cemetery. Today its map, which migrations, pilgrim and commercial caravans have enlarged, resembles a camel's head that groups the activities of residents around the location of the eye. The density of population in the city center (its eye) reaches 193 individuals per square kilometer, whereas overall the density is 6.7 per square kilometer. A vast desert surrounds this eye, limiting the population density of all life forms.[*]

The camel kneels chest-first at the edge of Wadi al-Nisa' ("Women's Valley"), which was created by geologic movements and which is surrounded by a thick, fan-shaped rise of boulders, gypsum, and sand, deposited by flows from the southern desert, the northern swampy lakes, and rivers that no longer exist. The women of Basra used to frequent the valley to gather truffles. The spring rain would cause the earth to explode with white mushrooms and red khalasi truffles. Here Wa'il ibn Qasit passed by the tent of a woman called Asma' bint Duraym. Finding her alone, he expressed an interest in her. She said, "By God, if you are interested in me, I shall certainly summon my lions." Her lions were her nine sons, whom she had named after beasts of prey. In this manner the valley acquired its name: Valley of the Predators.

Atop a hundred geologic layers of prior devastation, Darb al-Kha'if ("Scared Man's Track") will lead a fleeing prisoner from the Naqrat al-Salman Penitentiary to a valley in al-Basiya. Then a Bedouin granddaughter of Asma bint Duraym will grant him shelter before the desert of freedom can seize him.

Fear causes roads to fork, whereas death unites them. Like a lamp suspended from the neck of the celestial bull, the constellation of the Pleiades was gleaming like a spear held high over the Valley of the Predators, beckoning al-Zubayr ibn al-Awwam, who was returning from the Battle of the Camel. It was watching over the horseman, who was trailed by his servant, but al-Ahnaf ibn Qays sent a man after

---

[*] These numbers are from a 1973 census; see: Da'ud Jasim al-Rabi'i, *Qada' al-Zubayr: dirasa fi al-jughrafiya al-bashariya* (Basra: Markaz Dirasat al-Khalij, 1978). (A)

al-Zubayr. The man caught up with al-Zubayr. When it was time to perform his prayers, al-Zubayr turned his back on this scout, who speared him. The lamp shook from the splintering of armor, and the sands lapped up the blood of the Pleiades. The servant buried his master's corpse in the valley and continued on his way until he emerged from the depression. Then, as he looked back down it, stucco dwellings were revealed to him, breaking through the sand and rising around the grave. The city would not be completed until nine centuries later.

Umar ibn al-Khattab desired that there should be no barrier between the caliphal capital of al-Madina and the new military city of Basra. This wish bequeathed a name, which collected to it the ends of roads. Umar's city, however, to guard against its final death, carried its name away and bounded twenty-one kilometers deeper into the southern plain, leaving behind as a shadow over its ruins its other name, which was "al-Zubayr." We would assume that what remains of it is a brittle, white foundation floating in the space of the years, had the wisdom of the road not intervened to show us the solidarity of the tomb and well at the ancient site. The tomb gave its name to the road's extension, and the well became the foundation for the continued existence of the place. The tombstones and the domed sepulchers of al-Zubayr, Talha, al-Hasan al-Basri, Ibn Sirin, Utba, Anas ibn Malik, and the Basran dead quench their thirst from deep, sweet springs, and the city of the dead rests solidly on layers of marine sedimentation.*

When Ibn Battuta arrived in Basra in AH 728, he witnessed only a few men in the encampment of the Haram ibn Sa'd and in that

---

* Abd al-Rahman Tahmazi has pointed out the hold that the dead exercise over the subconscious of the living (a hold over the purport of life) evidenced by the similarity of one of the markers for the dead (erecting graves for the dead) to one of the markers of life (the settling of embryos in wombs). This provocative thought continues to provide harmonious new insights. See his article: "Inqilab al-dhakira/Radhat al-la-shu'ur," *Majalla al-aqlam*, 1990/5. (A) of the Bani Hudhayl. The tribes of the other three encampments had moved across the Ubulla River to a new location on the Shatt al-Arab. This migration ignored the tomb born on the camel's hump in the Valley of the Predators. Al-Zubayr shunned the river culture, feeling satisfied with the desert. As it entered its shell of sand, however, it withheld from historic neglect the mother city's bricks and plaster. The winds also overlaid the sediment covering the ruins with the latest seeds and voices from the assemblies, so that its Bedouin sash became embroidered with these fashions.

The mud-brick wall called for a pickax to demolish it. The new pickaxes pluck from the air the echoes of the ancient ones. The smooth baked brick was applied as first aid to gashes in the Friday mosque's and the ancient city wall's bricks that the first Zubayrians used to build their dwellings. There remained of the ruler's residence and the adjoining mosque only a column and the remnants of a wall. These revealed the vast cycle of destruction that had enveloped governor, commander, judge, shaykh, landowner, and merchant. The last section of al-Zubayr's city wall, which was built in 1802 to extend the white dwellings as a transient, limitless façade confronting the desert in order to absorb caravans from distant roads, has collapsed. People arriving in the city noticed an evolution in the name inscribed on the white wall as the valley evolved from tomb to hamlet to date-processing center to market to exchange to municipal council. A city—at the edge of the land—is distinguished by its six emblems: camel, rain, well, tomb, hawk, and desert.

The children of the first Najdi migrants, who settled al-Zubayr in the first and second decades of the twelfth century AH built towers outside the city wall in order to protect their commercial caravans. The city then retreated inside the wall, leaving the tower sentries to face the limestone mountain of Sinam, which is rounded like a pale, distant wing. Isolation and a vast sweep of land trained them to read the sky's pathways, which are delimited by stars, and to gather information from the returning bells that shook on the necks of mounts flowing across the waterless wastes. The land here was like Ha'il's, which al-Hamdani compared to the hand of a welcoming host who sees in it a rider half a day away. The caravan passed beneath the eyes of the sentries, who were experienced in judging the route taken by the caravan and the tribe guiding it. The tower offered views in all four directions where the routes split off. The longest route ran through Wadi al-Batin via two trails. The first trail sent the caravans of al-Hajjaj off to Mecca in a southwestern direction, passing by al-Ruk'a and al-Hafr, for more than a thousand kilometers, and carried migrants from the cities of Najd in the opposite direction for eight hundred kilometers. The second was used by the Bedouins when they traveled from their homelands around the wells and grazing lands of al-Basiya to trade for grain in the markets of al-Zubayr. This grain route headed south to the hills of Jarishan and then turned east toward al-Zubayr, a distance of 195 kilometers.

The desert is an ancient book over which fingers have moved, wearing down its pages after pens etched its surfaces. The desert is revelation, light, emptiness, a voice, and a sign. Balzac said, "The desert is God without mankind." It abounds with tombstones of buried guides and the monuments of departed tribal shaykhs. There you find maps of branching paths drawn by commercial representatives who served in the desert for long years.* Today, however,

---

* Two of the most important books written about Iraq's three deserts are: Abd al-Jabbar al-Rawi, *al-Badiya*, and Makki al-Jamil, *al-Badu wa al-qaba'il al-rahhala fi-l-'Iraq*. I relied on the map found in the first book to establish the southern desert route. (A)

these are lost routes across which legendary camels walked during a long day. The maps mark the locations of wells, places where rain-water may accumulate, pools, valleys, hills, mountains, the tribes' grazing and camping areas, which wind-borne sand has effaced. We lack the ability of the Bedouin (whether a Shammari, an Inizi, a Mutayri, a Dhufayri, or a Salbi) to use our imagination to differentiate between lightning out of a rain-filled cloud (al-muzna) and its fraud-ulent, dry look-alike (al-makhila) when each lightning bolt strikes at a distance, apparently promising a downpour, to allow us to follow the footprints of the Scared Man's Track, which links al-Salman to al-Basiya. We call it the Fugitive's Path, because it welcomed a prisoner who was able to escape from imprisonment in Naqrat al-Salman and covered a dreadful distance of 345 kilometers.

The prisoner drew his escape map on an empty water skin, substi-tuting the topography of freedom for that of fear. He spent a black night inside the cave of a rock-cut well overlooking the prison below. He could hear the dripping water and suppressed clamor of the well. It was the first well on his map. The chill of autumn was in the air, and Canopus had left his yawning wives in Ursa Minor. The prison was a pit open to the sky, and each prisoner in it felt linked to one star that was always visible and to another that was only briefly visible. These two guided him to the lunar phases associated with them and to stars that were in sequence with them. Summer was the time of exodus for the constellation Scorpio, and winter was a time for conjunc-tion with Andromeda. Fall brought stars that trailed after each other like camels linked with luminous ropes. The fugitive delighted in the heavenly caravan and appealed for the North Star's assistance to set the course for him toward Mecca. He filled his water skin with water from the well before sunrise and took one of the two trails into which the road marked on his map forked. Two-thirds of the route was rugged and deserted. The second well was concealed in a place with many rocks. Two worm-eaten wooden posts marked it. The bucket was cut off, and its twisted-wool rope was coiled on the lip of the circular well. He dropped a stone, which was lost in the well's void along with the sun's straight rays. He had a small quantity of water left from the other bitter well, enough for traveling half the next day. He kept moving until at sunset he reached the way station at the end of the terrifying part of the road. He spent the night on the far side of a low, rocky hill. Between him and the well was a depression where shallow water collected. Travelers had prepared a walled hiding place with stones and lit a fire in a pile of wood, which had not all burned. The fugitive collected the remaining firewood and lit it. When the fire died out, he wrapped himself in his cloak and lay down, after devouring a handful of dates from his sack. Then he thought he heard footsteps approaching. His limbs trembled and he felt uneasy until a cold, red dawn banished the whispered suggestions of the dark. On examining the sand that morning, he discovered animal tracks circling the hill. The multiplicity of the tracks showed him how alone he was and the dearth of sounds or words made him feel forgotten by man and beast alike. No patrol intercepted him and no camel crossed his path. Meanwhile his map was bringing him to wells, catchment basins, and sidr trees in sequence and guiding him toward the final valley of salvation. The established name for this valley was Ghar al-Sabil, and after it came the grazing land of Takid, where he hoped to find a caravan of nomadic Arabs. The land beyond this sandy grazing area spread out for a distance of seventy-five kilometers before al-Basiya. The fugitive, however, whose sense of direction was exhausted, veered off far to the east. His feet began to drag, and his wounds were covered with clotted blood and black scabs. The sun's reflections off the boulders and sand dunes made his eyes see red specters. Based on the evidence of the short columns of stone erected as monuments by the Bedouins in places where they had camped, sundials drew his cloak toward those who had traveled to God's grazing lands. Hope's compass in his head encouraged him to think he was heading in the right direction, even as the sun's random dials dragged him down the labyrinth's paths. Thus he found himself overlooking a pastoral valley not located on his map, and his unsteady eyes observed a single, isolated tent. Unable to bear the wounds of his flight any longer, he dashed toward the spacious depression like a madman. When he regained consciousness, he heard the desert echo a humming sound and observed—from where he now lay in the middle of the tent—a woman churning milk outside. With her gestures she stirred his spirit, which was refreshed by the fanning of a cold breeze. He learned from her that the place where he had landed on her carpet was called al-Kusayr, that it lay to the east of al-Basiya, and that she was a shepherdess, whose people had left her alone with her child while they went off for provisions. She poured him some coffee. Then she put a knife on the hearth to sterilize before she cauterized the wounds on his feet. She said, "Like rain, strangers are a gift from God." That evening she prepared herbal poultices with which she covered his cauterized wounds. She did not ask him about himself but deduced—from his ravings about the labyrinth's sundials, the restraint of a female jackal that had found him one night in a cave, a row of sidr trees, a hare's den, and a deep cell like a pit—that his daze had driven sandstorms into his head, burying the Scared Man's Track and the prison to which that trail led. This is all he remembered from his nightmare. Some days later the guest joined a caravan that was heading from al-Kusayr to al-Basiya, al-Zubayr, and then the land of God. That was a gift of the pain of the cauterizing knife, a cup of camel milk, and the hospitality of a solitary Bedouin woman. Freedom is something that is earned like the butter that is separated from the milk in the churn and like water that is drawn from a well in an arid wasteland.

I do not intend to buttress the preceding story of flight with real-life sources, for I wove it from the oral testimony of many different people. Perhaps one in ten was successful in narrating something true to life. For this reason I rely for backing on literature in following the paths of flight and deriving a moral for them. The prisoner from Salman was fated to avoid meeting any living creature throughout the long stages of his flight, although he wished he had the company of a female jackal, snake, or hare to remind him of human times, so that his waking nightmares caught only the shadows of the sun's dials. Balzac's short story "A Passion in the Desert" relates a different fate for a Provençal soldier who served in the French invasion of Egypt. Taken prisoner by Bedouins, Mamluks, or Moroccans, he was able to escape on a horse he stole from his captors. He sought refuge in the desert, but the horse perished from exhaustion. Then the soldier retired to a defenseless hill surrounded by extensive sand dunes like the blazing blade of a sword. Growing on top were some date palms with delicious, fresh dates, and flowing at its foot was a pure spring. The fugitive soldier embraced the hill with delight and congratulated himself on this refuge, which would protect him till soldiers from the expedition or passersby rescued him. The soldier, expecting that wild animals from the desert would be attracted to the spring, chopped down a dead palm trunk to block the entrance to a cave where he would bed down once night fell. The fugitive's hunch proved correct, for the cave was the lair of a desert princess.

He awoke in the dark to hear the breathing of a terrifying animal. In the moonlight, he identified it as a leopardess, her mouth spattered with blood. The leopardess turned toward him. Then terror froze the soldier's hand, which had drawn his sword for combat. Contrary to his expectations, the leopardess approached and indicated that like any other hostess she desired her guest's comfort. He made so bold as to caress her back with his hand. She submitted to his caresses and showed such affection and sympathy that his apprehensions were allayed and he treated his eyes to the complete enjoyment of her youthful body. She submitted voluntarily to his fingers as they fondled her svelte form while he continued to admire her beauty and youthfulness. She was as lovely as a woman experiencing comparable passion, jealousy, and suspicions. In his loneliness and longing for another human being, he made her his girlfriend and named her after his sweetheart Mignonne.* He grew convinced that this woman's spirit dwelt in her, and this conviction strengthened his attachment to her. The way he saw it, the desert was populated by a creature that had renounced its savagery in order to keep him company in his solitude, which had been transformed into enjoyment replete with the desert's beauty, pleasures, music, and colors. The leopardess became increasingly devoted to her master, whom she rescued from a quicksand pit into which he fell while trying to escape from her. As love's blaze intensified, though, the possibility for misunderstanding became more pronounced. In a moment of dalliance, the French soldier thought the leopardess meant to attack and plunged his dagger in her throat. The comrades who rescued him found him weeping as if he had lost a human companion whom he was unable to restore

---

* Latifa in Arabic. (T)

to life. Balzac asks the story's narrator what he found in the desert. The narrator, who was the love-struck soldier himself, says, ". . . everything, and nothing." When asked to explain, the man replies somewhat impatiently, ". . . it is God without mankind."*

The desert, which banishes blessings and beasts, leads them back to its pastures like a nursing she-camel and never tires of opening to the city a gate that is five centuries old. We will suppose that a caravan from the tribe of al-Zufayr is returning to meet with its inhabitants at the pond called Daym Khazim east of al-Zubayr. The water is drawn by a waterwheel from a sweet-water well dug in an orchard with a wall built around it. The fronds of date palms shade the pool's waters.† The caravan has provisioned itself at the city's market with what it needs for the coming winter season: dates, rice, flour, and cloth, which fill the saddlebags fastened to the riding camels. The men perform the dawn prayer in the mosque adjacent to the orchard, leaving their camels to drink from the elongated basin. Then they fill their water skins and attach them to the saddles of two powerful camels. The female camels twist their necks out of homesickness when they hear the call to prayer. (I turn my gaze to follow the camels arriving in the painting by al-Wasiti. Then I whisper in response to the sun and the sand.) The caravan reaches the depression called al-Birjisiya but does not stop at its wells. The sand dunes are tinted by morning's effusion, and the camels hurry forward, fleeing from their shadows that the sun accentuates. The caravan descends into Wadi al-Batin once it leaves al-Rank campsite and does not stop

---

* Honoré de Balzac, "A Passion in the Desert," *Short Stories*, T.R. Smith, ed. (New York: The Modern Library, no. 40, n.d.), 126. (T)

† The pool was constructed in the year AH 1314; then it was buried along with the valley of Daym Khazim, which fed rainwater to it, and a road was constructed there instead. See: Yusuf Ahmad al-Bassam, *al-Zubayr qabla khamsin 'aman* (Kuwait: al-Matba'a al-'Asriya, 1971). (A)

Muhammad Khudayyir

until it reaches a rainwater pool beneath a sidr tree. The Bedouins set their camels free to graze on the few bitter rimth weeds and thorny shrubs in a field where daisies bloom and posies interrupt the glum sands with their charm. They lighten the camels' loads and place in the shade of the sidr tree the howdah of a woman they are carrying to a desert doctor (slubi) in al-Zubayr. They invite the woman to reflect on the gifts of the first rain. She opens eyelids that illness has made heavy and offers thanks for this blessing even though her body is parched. They set off again so darkness will not catch them halfway down the valley. At sunset they make camp among the Jarishan hills in the valley's last pasturage before the northern turn to al-Basiya. Their dismounting creates a racket and the camels, kneeling beside the hills, raise a ruckus. Then night brings a moon that spreads light across the sands and restrains the knees of rowdy camels with delicate ropes.

One sand dune asks another, "Where is the word-weaver?"* The campfire's flame points to the circle of Bedouins, who have been drinking coffee from a small pot and have finished their repast with dates. When the flaming roots and branches diffuse a fragrance that the Najd breeze spreads, they begin to weave strands of talk into a discussion. Discourse is the essence of the tribe and its heart. Fire, flirtation, tobacco, poetry, and the rabab are the pegs of the night's vast tent. Talk, however, has top billing. This rope binds the tribe to the night's tent and the desert. The ear is the tongue's hostage and the heart is the spirit's absorbent sponge. Fragmentary sentences are exchanged and phrases fall one after another like dates until a man at the center takes control of the conversation's drift. He is now the weaver—a

---

* This turn of phrase appeared in *al-'Iqd al-farid* when Uthman ibn Sa'id asked a taciturn man riding in his boat about his profession and the man replied, "Word weaver." Ibn Abd Rabbih, *al-'Iqd al-farid* (Beirut: Dar Maktabat al-Hilal, 1986), 4:18. (A)

word-weaver—and the entertainer for those gathered around. His words lead them with language's plaited ropes, which he sends to their ears in successive, balanced, and upright phrases that influence the air and fall on the sand, which imbibes them as if absorbing drops of water. As the discourse charts its path, the words free themselves from the hold of both tongue and dialect and shed their torn husks. The voice is firm, smooth, and transits the throat, which has made a profession of speaking, on the way to the tongue, which tosses out words like smooth pebbles. The melody of the voice controls the Bedouins' spirits and toys with their ears the way night toys with their masters' tobacco-coated beards. The voice comes from every side. The desert is the speaker—the singer, sonorous and suppliant, transforming bodies, turning them over as they sleep, drugging them until they resemble the senseless creatures stretched out on their backs in paintings by Breughel.

Orientalist painters who spent time with desert Arabs were extra-ordinarily fond of depicting caravans at rest on heights overlooking Arab cities as well as scattered desert oases.* How could we dispense with the radiant yellow of the Orientalist watercolors? It envelops proud displays of artifacts (clothing, howdahs, and tents) around a spring or pond. The amber horizon foretelling dusk, the impending sunrise that announces a departure, the expanse and friction of the sand, the camel calling its mate, a stick to poke into the sand, the pure brown faces, and a hand raised to the eye that gazes at the horizon have sent these pictures to the museum of the eternal. The anonymous caravans in them still traverse the invisible desert, back and forth.

---

* In March 1982, the Mathaf Gallery, established in London in 1975, exhibited under the title "Lands Without Shadows" one hundred and fifty Orientalist paintings by travel and topo-graphic painters—of various nationalities—who traveled in Arab lands during the nineteenth century. The most famous of these were the Italians Rosati and Bartolini, the Englishmen Haag and Robertson, the Frenchman Gérôme, and the Austrian Deutsch. (A)

We pick for discussion the French artist Jean-Léon Gérôme's painting of three veiled Arab nomads on horseback. In it, extensive distances bring even peaks low, and each man is alone with his thoughts. One of the two horsemen in the foreground leans a long lance against his shoulder. A third figure trails them. He is wrapped in a red shawl that covers his head and body and hangs loosely over the flanks of his horse. The two men in front are slightly built Bedouins, and the colors of their splendid robes contrast with the expanse and dull color of the desert. We turn from them to inspect the red-clad horseman, whose identity is concealed. He is increasingly self-absorbed and turns as he advances. The Bedouin's intuition is a form of pure conjecture, certainty without proof, and experience refined by solitude and distance. Gérôme used some of that type of intuitive knowledge to paint this picture. He entered into it, for the third horseman is the painter, who has concealed his Christian identity beneath a red cloak and thrust himself into the painting among the tribal Arabs.

Wilfred Thesiger, in his book *Arabian Sands*, talks about a group of Bedouins he accompanied to explore the south of the Arab desert. They played a game like checkers with camel droppings. The great traveler, who was lying beneath the warm winter sun, watched this simple game with interest and delight. The game was far more valuable than any survey map he carried, for through it, he mastered the desert's mystery in brief, intriguing tidbits. Similar to this game, which was played in the sand, was the sand-writing traced by an elderly Bedouin with a thick, white beard. I read many regions in the lines of dots he dug with his fingers and the lines they divided into columns. The book of the desert is endless and does not merely hide the world in a grain of its sand, but each grain conceals a world, all by itself. When al-Ablaq, the fortress of Samuel ibn Adiya, constituted the heart of the desert, the world was an unknown region beyond its walls. After the sands buried the fortress, a Bedouin came and planted his staff in the sand covering it in order to mark the center of the world.

Al-Zubayr ibn Awwam used to say, "The world is Basra." This man had traveled from the middle of the Arabian peninsula to stand at the final fringe of the desert. There he encountered the city he considered the end of the world. The citizen of al-Zubayr today tugs on his tapered beard and contemplates the open border of the desert while whispering to himself, "Truly, al-Zubayr is a city that lies at the end of the world." He sees it as a city that is the size of a grain of sand and that rotates around the desert like a planet. Indeed, any similar oasis a Bedouin reaches, when his trip has exhausted him, seems to his eyes the end of the world. The Ka'ba in Mecca is the center, where all the earth's roads meet the sky. This cubical structure, which preserves beneath its black covering the true reality of the world, is God *with* people.

A long time has passed since the caravan of al-Zufayr set out, and the Bedouin's grandson has no hope of inheriting the word until another word-weaver enters the city. I noticed someone resembling him in the livestock market. My eye was confused, however, because in appearance and character he differed from the Bedouin who frequent the market with their erect bearing, flowing hair, coal-black beards, and gleaming white teeth.

In a story that Lamartine relates, Antar and his brother Shaybub meet an old hermit in the desert and accept his hospitality. When Antar asks the old man about his stooped way of walking, he replies, "'My youth has been lost on the earth, and I bend downward, as ever seeking to recover it there.'"*

---

* Alphonse de Lamartine, *Memoirs of Celebrated Characters (Le Civilisateur)* (New York: Harper & Brothers Publishers, 1856), vol. 3, 189. (T)

My old shaykh reminded me of this man. He had tied his donkey beneath the dome of al-Hasan al-Basri near the cemetery. He was a desert visitor who settled here and made his living by transporting clover on his donkey from nearby fields and selling it in the souk. As he led his donkey, he would search the ground for a riddle that the legend of the sand had cast at his feet or had buried in the shrine's circle and the curves of the conical minaret.

The word-weaver might have been a falconer I observed one morning at the far end of town, resting in a coffeehouse of a bus stop by the side of the desert road that leads to al-Nasiriya. The vehicle, which had a long wooden frame, was waiting for other passengers before departing. The falconer removed his sandals and curled up on the bench while holding a hooded Indian falcon, with its foot fastened by a double band to the man's leather glove. The falcon, which had its head covered, was probing with its hooked beak the intentions of its trainer, whose head was covered by a red kerchief. He was oblivious to the surroundings and to the Bedouin-style travel song that coiled around the passengers' necks like a sand viper. The falconer jumped off at the ruins of al-Khamisiya and paused for a moment to observe the cloud of sand that trailed after the wooden vehicle. Then he turned his eyes to a hawk soaring in the sky over the ruins, its wings unrestrained. My view of him fell away in the distance, as the road closed it off, and it disappeared forever. The driver lost his way on his return, and ancient castles were revealed to him on both sides of the lost road of Bilqis, Queen of Sheba. Tayma' drew the wheels toward it just as it attracts the speeding camel, which pays no attention when the large shadow of a bird passes over it.

In an old book about predatory birds, I read that a prince once grew angry at his falconer and banished the man to a castle deep in the desert. The falconer entreated his master to allow him to take a trained eagle to the castle with him, and the prince granted this request. The falconer was getting on in years—as was the eagle— and he wished to write a book about the characteristics of birds of prey he had used and trained. He adorned it with drawings portraying the different varieties, their characteristics, and the way they dived on their prey. The eagle sat on his perch, following his master's quill as it drew lines and pictures, until the appointed hour arrived. When the falconer died, the eagle disappeared and the book was carried to the prince, who suffered from insomnia and took his falconer's book to bed, where he became engrossed in reading it. The prince was amazed at the falconer's skill in narrating special moments in falconry and at his expertise in decorating the margins with pictures of birds of prey. Among these illustrations was an eagle, pulsing with vitality and beauty. The prince was startled to see the eagle's sharp beak and long striped wings. The letters twisted like black talons, and as the prince turned the pages, they fluttered like two terrifying wings that had broken free from his bed's canopy, which was embroidered with pictures of falconry, and then lit on his breast. The black talon edged closer to his heart, seeking to mangle it. When the prince finished reading the last page, drops of blood stained the edges of the book, which fell on his chest. The picture of the eagle, for its part, disappeared from its place in the manuscript.

There is a prophetic link between the falconer's eagle and the fish of Dino Buzzati, who writes about a maritime beast called "K" that would relentlessly follow the prey it selected until it was captured. In this story, the victim was a ship captain's son whom it had been following for fifty years. When the predator fish K and its victim—now a captain—were both growing old, in order to discover its mythic credo, the man decided to confront the predator rather than continue fleeing. Then it transpired that the fish was not trying to devour him but instead endeavoring to give him a rare maritime jewel. This myth is like the mirage that created the tales of the falconer's book. The sea is like the desert in that its will too is eternal. The wing that clips the edge of the fin that cleaves the wave's edge. Of Thamud and the Atlantic, only a comprehensive stillness survives, for sand dunes move as secretly as waves. The camel kneels after a journey through myths. Its hump is toward the desert and its muzzle toward the sea.

We return now to the shaykh and his donkey and find them still beneath the white dome and the conical minaret. Dusk has attracted to the shrine yesterday's voices, which circle around the remaining column of the Friday mosque. The mosque's prayer groups have dispersed, but early the next morning the old man, whose donkey is snoozing, listens to the returning whispers beneath the dome and a repetition of conversations like the clicking of prayer beads in the hands of al-Hasan al-Basri, Amr ibn al-Alla', Ibn Sirin, or al-Khalil— a long set of prayer beads made from date pits, hundreds of which are strung on a fine wool thread. The shaykh counts to the soft sound of the prayer beads the early mornings left to him in al-Zubayr's streets, markets, mosques, and cemetery. The tomb summons life's term, and wisdom summons the imagination. The remaining beads of life's span we will string on the lines of the following story.

You will definitely not find for sale in any city of the world Yemeni-type footwear better, more beautiful, and sturdier than those from al-Zubayr. Death, however, has begun to consume both the skilled craftsmen and their leather. For a long time some shops have made Yemeni footwear for barefoot visitors from the desert and for mourners who bury their dead in al-Zubayr's cemetery and then carry home handsome red shoes. That was before factory-made shoes became prevalent and the craft of piercing leather and of mending shoes was supplanted. When a cobbler died, his workshop closed. Thus when you passed through the old souk, you would find two out of three doors closed, their bolts rusty, and the wood decayed. Time continued to close one shop after another until the day arrived that only one aged shoemaker opened his door in the souk, but eventually his eyesight deteriorated and he lost touch with time and people. Since no one trusted this cobbler's work anymore, no barefoot person had commissioned him to make a pair of sandals for a long time. All the same he spent hours and days hunched over his dusty leathers, creating a pair of sandals. This was the last pair, one he was making for himself in preparation for a long journey on the rugged road to the other world.

The cobbler did not expect anyone to request the sandals on his bench, but when dark night had enveloped the old market with its gloom—since the only light shining through it was that from the lamp in the cobbler's shop, which remained open among the closed shops—a dusty man, who apparently had traveled from a distant land, appeared in the midst of the scent of old leather out of the silence of the nearby desert. The old man did not notice the visitor, who was wearing a shroud. Neither did he realize that this customer was dead, for the cobbler was busy sewing the final stitches in the leather of his sandals with his feeble fingers. The stranger took a seat on a low bench and waited for the cobbler to finish. Then he seized the sandal from his hands and pounded him over the head with it. This was the final, fatal blow. After that, the visitor disappeared with the pair of sandals. Like any other dead person, the visitor had a face that was burnished like a piece of scrubbed leather. For this reason, the cobbler's eyes did not recognize him before the sparkle of life left them.

Anyone who quickly traverses the souk in the dark of the night will see a slender thread of light stealing from cracks in the panels of the closed door, because the cobbler's spirit is busy making another pair of sandals, since in order to enter their world the dead need red leather footwear, handcrafted by a cobbler from al-Zubayr.

Mobile   City

A PASSENGER ON THE night train confronts this riddle: did cities and their train stations create trains—or did trains create cities and their stations?

Since my first train trip in the 1960s, the train has disclosed to me one of the laws of perception, portrayal, and creative writing, because if you remember how fields spring forth at dawn with the rising sun, how the earth's undulations gradually advance, and how life surges before you in those isolated places, which then rapidly retreat behind you, you will discover—like me—one of the unpublicized private laws for writing short stories, for here thought emerges and takes shape, slowly at first and then quickly. Then the real and the symbolic fade and quickly vanish behind you—just as scenes emerge, gradually take shape, and then vanish from the train's windows. We should not be content to borrow perfect rules for literary composition from other writers; we must instead discover its principles for ourselves. Thus there are laws we do not normally perceive that reveal themselves to us in moments of great surprise in times and places far-removed from cities when we are on trains traveling here and there, night and day.

I need to replay for your eyes scenes of the fields as they appear from a train window in broad daylight and to remind you of the shrubs that bend in response to its speed, the livestock that are cast behind us, the spreading plume of smoke, the roar of the wheels over bridges that span rivers and gorges, the whistle that draws boys with disheveled hair from their huts to witness precipitous, reverberating life with tilted faces and drowsy eyes. I remind you of dawn's bake-ovens, of birds soaring over gleaming swamps, and of the numerous villages and cities the train leaves behind.

The green third-class carriages that played host to my body during many nights of my continuing voyage had hard wooden seats with racks opposite for luggage. I slept during these trips on seats and racks, using my suitcase as a pillow. In those carriages I met beggars, vendors, soldiers, and travelers climbing aboard or getting off in stations with no known name or form, lost in the desert or in a succession of farms. I would like to recount for you here some events, anecdotes, and light tragedies as I describe for you what I saw on trains during the 1960s. I really want to write a book of thousands of pages about strangers encountered in this nocturnal, mobile life. These trains are like fleeting banquets that cast you into a whirlpool of sorrows or send a chortle to your throat, if they do not drive you to flee to distant farms. The train created unbreakable fraternal bonds between me and those strangers—brothers of the night and travel, brothers of the unknown life that settles in one place only to depart for somewhere else. Anyone who—like me—has felt human ties dissolve among the brethren during our long nights when trains thunder forward plucks these ties back from the silent night by force.

The black train twitches and then belches steam. It bids farewell to the Ma'qil Station in Basra and to the setting sun with a prolonged wail, pulling behind it lengthy green wagons. After it has passed twenty principal and branch stations, the Baghdad West Station appears with morning's harbingers. In its daily trip, the train traverses 569 kilometers on the narrow-gauge railroad line (three feet, three-and-a-half inches wide) that the British occupation army laid in 1914 along the Euphrates as a replacement for the German line, which was established in 1910. Only one of the bituminous-coal-fired German trains continued in operation until it was withdrawn from service in 1951, when it was displayed as a historic monument outside the international terminal in Baghdad. Ownership of the railway line and its rolling stock was transferred to the Iraqi government in 1935. The line was updated with standard-gauge tracks, and diesel-powered steam engines were imported so that the indefatigable travels of this viper, which dragged its heavy, steel segments between the ancient cities of the southern plains, could continue. The train was preceded by its wail, which the sand dunes, lakes, and fields absorbed while the low domes of residences for the railway workers and their supervisors sucked up the echo.

When the incoming train passes Baghdad's second station (al-Shu'ayba), travelers see flares of natural gas from the refineries. This first landmark of a trip from Baghdad will be the last landmark that welcomes the train on its return to Basra. The conical dome of the tomb of Zumurrud Khatun, the wife of the Caliph al-Mustadi' bi-Amr Allah, is the last landmark for the trip through time between the cities of the fertile Euphrates. Torches and dim lamps soar far in front of the wagons that speed along the stages of the route, but the sun's disc will confront the train before it pulls out of the twelfth or thirteenth station. It is the same sun that rose on travelers in the deserts and on the roads of foreign cities and that so startled camels that they rushed off—foaming and startled—with their loads, welcoming the legendary face of this sphinx. The red disc rose from the plain of Babil with its towers, surprising the locomotive, which rushed from ancient Ur to the cities of the future with terrifying speed.

Nature has submitted to the will of man while decreasing his means of subjecting time to his imaginative whims and emotional tantrums, although nature has assisted him in inventing devices that remind him of time. Museums, airplanes, and clocks are time machines that traverse the space of memory, going and coming. Bridges and railroad stations are stationary observatories (in the arched space of cities and railroads) to which are entrusted the observation of rivers and of trains speeding through time's tunnel. Stand on a bridge to watch the Tigris flow past and remember the Mirabeau Bridge on the River Seine and Apollinaire's poem about it in order to feel the passing days, hours, and minutes.

> *Beneath the Mirabeau Bridge flows the Seine*
> *And our loves.*
> *Must it remind me*
> *That pain has always preceded joy?*
> *So let the night fall and the hour strike;*
> *The days pass and I remain.*
> *Hand in hand, let us stand face to face*
> *While under*
> *The bridge of our arms flows*
> *A tired wave of unending looks.*
>
> . . . .
> . . . .

Love passes like this flowing water.

        . . . .

How slow life is
And how violent hope!
        So let the night fall and the hour strike;
        The days pass and I remain.[*]

The old stationmaster stands watching a train as it approaches his isolated station that lies in the open countryside between two cities. Holding their red and green lanterns, the signalmen also notice the fleeting passage of the express night train's lighted windows. They see a man squeezed into a corner of a carriage. This man, for whom I propose the name Isa ibn Azraq, quickly shoots past the stations. Its lamps retreat into the distance, falling like prayer beads into the bowl of the night. Against this fixed reference point, the stations of a man's life and its shaky lighthouses burst forth in the darkness of his memory. The aged stationmaster will receive (as one of the night's marvels) the thoughts of the passenger on the train. We can illustrate these with stanzas from the poem "The Thoughts of Isa ibn Azraq En Route to Difficult Tasks" by the poet Mahmud al-Barikan:

Hour after hour I look apprehensively
At the countryside and the stations. Am I
Asleep? Have I been wrested from my world?
I still see ghosts: people who wave,
Run, laugh, board, and disembark,

---

[*] For the complete French original and an alternative English translation see Guillaume Apollinaire, *Alcools*, trans. Anne Hyde Greet (Berkeley & Los Angeles: University of California Press, 1965), 14–15. (T)

Muhammad Khudayyir

> *As though they were nothing more than ghosts of memories;*
> *As though they were nothing more than a crowd of shadows*
> *In a strange dream.**

I revive in my memory the scene of a train hurtling forward without regard to destination, an arrow gone astray, swimming in the emptiness of the open countryside. A continual forward thrust and the exchange of stations and passengers allow my imagination to suggest an exchange of roles. I am in the very seat used by the coach's previous passenger, and he was preceded by the other passengers who transited the same station my train is approaching. I rely here on a selection from a 1987 diary of a northbound train trip. I know I was once again approaching a legend (al-Nasiriya) and not issues relating to it or to its appearance, when I observed from the train window the clock of the station that had recently been erected. The station's clock—what a surprise—was on the blink, and I sensed that time had stopped outside the train. This train, which had passed the lakes surrounding Suq al-Shuyukh, was approaching al-Nasiriya. Then, in my consciousness, I heard a medley of sounds of a city I had observed seventeen years earlier while cooling my heels in that station for the southbound train one evening in 1962.

At that time, passengers were waiting for a train that would carry them from the branch station in Ur to the city's principal station, which was ten kilometers distant. On the return side, they were waiting for the train from Baghdad to carry them to Basra from this suburban station. Normally their wait would not last till after midnight. In Ur, there was a large hall where travelers sat

---

* Mahmud al-Barikan wrote this poem in 1958 and published it in Basra in the magazine *al-Fikr al-hayy*, no. 2. (A)

on stone benches while vendors selling tea, grilled meat, cigarettes, and newspapers circulated through the room, which was filled with soldiers, policemen, strangers, and refugees searching for warmth and human companionship. That night I quit the warm, crowded waiting room for the station's courtyard, which fused with the cold night. Freight cars were standing on the tracks, stars were glittering brightly, the night was clear and calm, and I was gripped by a violent tremor of solitude and alienation. Over there, a city had forsaken us. It was sleeping now, while we stayed up late to avoid missing the last train. When I returned to the waiting room, I was confronted by a mixed group of travelers, who were surrounded by smoke, and by their reciprocal breathing, souls, and words, which were critical of the city's rejection. Radio songs eroded hearts of stone and lit the fires of love in Ur in an atmosphere reminiscent of a day in the ancient hall of that Sumerian city's temple, on the debris of which the station was built.

I can tell you for certain that this waiting room was one of the real-life inspirations for the vision of Iraq that inspired my first short stories. I remember—in addition to the waiting room—markets that attracted nomadic Arabs with their camels and herds of sheep, a bowed, metal bridge over the Euphrates, a restaurant where the owner stood at the door inviting people who passed through the market to dine, a public bath with a large pool, a coffeehouse outside the city where a rare tape recorder played songs of the countryside and of the gypsies, an old palace, a mounted-police headquarters, a bookstore, and a cinema where women sat on one side and men on the other. In this movie theater, tea was sold and films from the 1950s were shown. The allergic ticket collector, who was subject to fits of sneezing, would return tickets to the window to be resold.

Images of this city—like a herd of camels crossing from one end of the bowed bridge to the other—crowded before my eyes.

Returning to original sources is difficult, even if those sources are scenes and images drawn from years spent in major cities like al-Nasiriya. Alas! The second viewing of those original sites will not be thrilling. Apparently the clock that hangs on their stations stopped when you departed.

In 1964 I settled as a teacher for a school in the village of al-Aridiyat, which is near al-Ramitha. Both places are linked to the history of tribal resistance to the British occupation. Pale-green fields surrounded the school, and a dirt road, which ran parallel to the large police station and a few homes for railway workers, separated it from the village's railway station. We did not know where our pupils' homes were located, for these were hidden by a bend of the Euphrates River, which ran east of the school.

There were five of us teachers living in the house attached to the school. Our bedroom was inside another large room. We would take refuge in the house at sunset. Lying on our beds, we would talk by lantern light. We kept one another company for days on end, suffocated by the overwhelming bonds that united us: the darkness, the feeble light—since we neglected to clean the lantern glass—our own smell, the inflections of our voices, the hopes confined inside us, and our terse, deliberate words, which we uttered slowly. There were no independent boundaries for our attitudes or pleasures, for these were all the same, whether mixed, minced, or cooked in our blackened pot. When we felt oppressed by these limitations, we would brag about the most trivial things. In the inner room, our five closely packed beds, which had loose springs and filthy mattresses indented by our bodies, the walls on which we had inscribed our thoughts, the silent oil lamp, the barking of dogs, the calls of wild birds in the desolate fields around the house, the sounds of the night, and then the whistle of the train as it approached the station—all these reminded us of our isolation and of our physical impotence in this place, which was a theater for a bitter struggle and for the heroic, nationalist resistance against occupation. The ghosts of our pupils, with their lean fingers clutching pieces of chalk, would finally appear as hungry messengers to rescue us from this siege.

When we went to school in the morning we were surprised to find fifty pupils spread across its grassy yard. Scrawny and destitute, they lacked any vitality and did not play together or pick quarrels with teachers. Regardless of their problems, they were more experienced than we were with the path that cut through the fields and passed derelict waterwheels. Each morning they carried their books and notebooks with torn covers, walking for hours without any gaiety, and finally entered the schoolyard, which was open in every direction. Once they left and disappeared, we withdrew to our room and retreated into self-absorption until morning the next day. We lived for their sake, just as the master of the nearby station lived for the sake of his daily train.

At a preordained moment of the night, the beds around mine shook and we awoke to the whistle of the train as it rapidly approached the village's station, the squeal of the wheels' friction against the tracks, and the hiss of the steam. Then we would hear the clamor of the passengers and the exchange between the stationmaster, the train's engineer, his crew, the guards, and the night's strangers. We would wait for the train's arrival and monitor from a distance that genial, nightly reunion.

We did not live for nothing. We lived for the sake of known or delayed goals, for brief or transitory special moments. One of us lived for a goal to which he had dedicated his whole life. The five of us in the room, the stationmaster out there—we had our moment that we anticipated for a specific time. When it arrived, each of us would say to himself, "This is the moment I live for."

In *Terre des hommes* by Saint-Exupéry, an old sergeant waits with a handful of men in a desert redoubt for the caravan that brings provisions to the fort every six months. The sergeant, at the moment of meeting, wishes to clink glasses with the captain of the arriving convoy and say, "'Here's luck!' to a man who has just jumped down from the back of a camel. Wait six months for this great moment."*

The sergeant's widely spaced moments in the desert are as epic as the brief moments of the stationmaster. Each man lives for these moments. They cannot restrain themselves from releasing a stifled cry in the face of the hope that explodes in front of them like a spring in the desert of their lives, which are arid and extensive: "Oh! Yes, yes, this is the moment we live for." We would meet our fifty pupils the next morning, and the master of the nearby railway station would be watching for the arrival of his moving goal late that night.

---

* Antoine de Saint-Exupéry, *Wind, Sand and Stars*, trans. Lewis Galantière (New York: Reynal & Hitchcock, 1939), 131–32. (T)

The air in the compartment was filled with stifling cigarette smoke. The chatter of the passengers and the screaming of the children made me feel peevish and prevented me from resting or relaxing. The thud of stumbling feet, the passengers packed in the aisle, and the alarming congestion all made me intensely uncomfortable, and for this reason I kept moving about nervously and could not get comfortable in my seat.

When the hubbub subsided a bit, the wail of a bereaved woman past fifty was heard in the long carriage. She had thrown herself at the feet of the passengers with sorrowful abandon and had carelessly tossed ahead of her a basket coated with black bitumen and filled with heaps of dirty bags and ancient clothes that gave off a disagreeable odor. The woman was incapable of restraining her choking tears. She screamed wretchedly and her painful, muffled moan cut short the travelers' conversations and restrained their tongues. She was weeping agonizingly for her only son, a young man who had died in a distant, gloomy Basra hospital. She was blowing her nose and wiping the tips of her fingers with her rough blue garment as she recited a mournful folk chant and beat her left knee with her hand. Then she rose—feeble, diffident, choked up, and anonymous. When I lifted my head a little, I noticed that another woman seated not far from me had leaned her weak, sorrowful head against a closed window as her ailing eyes released two streams of silent, sympathetic tears. She had found in weeping for this bereaved woman and her woes some release from her own repressed pains. Her aging heart had embraced these suppressed, buried pains.

Muhammad Khudayyir

This passage describing the carriage of sorrows is from Mahmud Abd al-Wahhab's short story "The Northbound Train for Baghdad," which contains a collection of scenes set in the train of the 1950s. It was published in the magazine *al-Adab* (Literature) early in 1954. The eyes of an inexperienced, sensitive student, who was heading for Baghdad to pursue his higher education, observed these scenes. The student's emotions also took in the travelers' faces, discussions, accents, claims, complaints, mirth, suffering, and their need for solidarity and camaraderie. From precise description, revelatory dialogue, and attention to the sensitive soul's anxious fears about the tragedies and pains surrounding it, we gain an understanding of an exemplary, mobile slice of life in a vast, stationary reality. The linked sentiments and realizations gradually progress from hatred to compassion and then to a comprehension of how rough and difficult life can be.

My eyes were fastened on the dying, dust-covered lamp, which was being energetically and agilely bombarded by raging insects, struggling and crowding against one another. I sensed that the train had begun to tilt until it threatened to tip over, and intermingling, contending images appeared to my mind's eye. I raised my hand to my heavy head and my straining eyes. The train was diligently traversing this desert, heedless of the dark, the distance, and the howl of jackals. My head fell between my shoulders and I dozed off. From time to time I would force my eyes open to see heads that were wounded, bowed, rounded, and dancing as well as the trembling lamp, next to which there was a bit of wood on which was written in Arabic and English: "Occupancy: 64 seated." I finally woke up and found that the sun was spreading its light over the earth, which looked thoroughly desolate. The carriage was almost empty. The wounded, bereaved woman had gotten off at Ur, even though I could still imagine I saw her slumbering in a mournful heap. Now the languid government employee seemed submerged as he slipped into the human current with his wife and child. The man from Baghdad still continued to prattle on as sincerely and enthusiastically as ever.

Just as the demands of travel brought together these unusual and contrasting personalites beneath the railroad car's feeble light, this slice of life from the coach proved the validity of the notion that every Iraqi has the potential to become a storyteller who can narrate a tale. My travels with various groups of people and my experiences in joining in their assemblies have underscored this hypothesis and charged it with certainty, vitality, and enjoyment. For a story to gain a listener's attention, it should not allow the thread of events to slacken. As it develops with subplots, and as different aspects of the story intertwine, it should not permit any gaps or sunlight between its words. The short story is a property granted to an unusual type of traveler, whose innocent, conscious eagerness for it never ceases in a crush of human beings. In my quiver—that of a traveler excited about exchanging roles—is a passage I plucked from the midst of a traveling slice of life in a train of the 1960s. I will relate this with some of the immediacy of feeling that overwhelmed me when I observed it for the first time, although I hope to narrate it objectively.

At that time, I truly was a moody man who lacked confidence in his failing memory. For that reason, I did what any man does: he persists in collecting pictures of artists like himself. My album included three faded photos of the rustic singer Khudayri Abu Aziz, going back to the days of his youth. I cut them out of newspapers that had begun to publish pictures of the singer after he retired from singing in his sunset years. The first picture showed him with a friend, wearing a head cloth with its ropes. In the second, he appeared bareheaded in the days when he was a policeman, entertaining his superiors in a boat making its way through the lakes. Then, once he moved to the broadcasting house, the third photo portrayed him as an actor in a film. None of the three photos, however, was a good likeness of Khudayri, who had numerous, legendary visages. By then I had created an imaginary portrait of Khudayri, gathering its elements from the faces of the villagers and Bedouins the train cast out at stations and plucked up from them, from the patrons of working-class coffeehouses, and from the visages of rural women, visitors at shrines, shepherds, and farmers. Of course, no imaginary portrait would resemble the face of the singer, who was thrown out of the train one summer night in a small station halfway between al-Samawa and al-Nasiriya. I am certain that no photographer captured the sad, averted face that was imprinted across representative Friday holidays, summer fields, wintry rural streets, and the day-spanning dawn. What camera will capture only the face of the singer of the new, small cities and omit the cloves of garlic and dried okra hanging from ceilings, the jugs of water, ovens, baskets, wooden mortars, millstones, spades, scythes, daggers, feather pillows, wool spindles held by old women basking in the sunshine beside dogs struggling to stay awake, small birds impaled on skewers, the sun slipping through skylights, the tranquility of small bridges, hornet nests, sloughed-off snake skins, the sparkle of rings on hennaed fingers, gold pins in long scarves—all of which appear in the background of the singer's image? When I was ten, I walked along a twisting lane at noon. My shirt was soiled by pomegranate, grass, and flower stains, and my bare toes were burned by the lane's fine dirt. The most forbidden images passed through my mind, causing me to sing. At that time, Khudayri's voice was linked to the large, elongated box of the vehicle of the mobile cinema. This vehicle, which had a bellowing loudspeaker, would park, from one month to the next during the summer, in an empty square that had originally been a dump. Boys had removed the rubbish and turned the area into a soccer field. The show began after sunset, when a cloth was stretched between two metal poles. Before the film's reels rolled and imagination's rays shot forth, songs would boom out of the vehicle's speaker for an hour. The movies were educational health films, and little in them concerned the unknown life of the peoples of Asia and Africa. Women were quicker than men to appear once they heard the songs. Farid al-Atrash would sing, "I wish I were a bird," Abd al-Wahhab would sing, "Oh Steam Engine," and the youthful Khudayri would sing, "Hey, Uncle Rose Vendor," while keeping time with his fingers. These songs were repeated from one Friday to the next in front of Primus stoves, over cradles on roof terraces, and at the river landings of dwellings. All the same, I repeat that any studio glossy or fantasy portrait would pale in comparison with the verisimilitude of the picture the night swallowed in that forlorn station lost among all the stations along the route.

It was a stifling night and there was a crush of people on a third-class carriage. Travelers were stretched out in the aisles and squeezed onto the racks with the luggage. Beggars were attempting to force their way between the bodies, and cigarette smoke was collecting in a quivering curtain that enveloped people's faces and prevented the ceiling lamp's light from illuminating their features. (Notice that

I am calling to mind the atmosphere of Mahmud Abd al-Wahhab's train coach.) Then a throaty voice was heard, cutting through the envelope of smoke. The travelers' tumult died away, and necks turned toward a villager who was crammed with his wife and daughter into a narrow space by the compartment door. He began to sing. This village man was pouring his vagrant lifeblood into a modal abudhiya. It twisted as much as the railway tracks in the dark of the night, growing fainter and then louder. It would melt and then solidify before bursting forth in a pure grief that united the hearts of the strangers of the night and shook their inner beings, turning them inside out like the lining of an overcoat. The villager concluded his abudhiya with the famous refrain, "The express train left me wandering in the night." His wife was gazing at his face with appalling sorrow while all the travelers, who were being jolted by the motion of the swaying train, listened attentively. The train's speed decreased. Then it stopped at a station. This was a small station, one of those lost in the desert. The villager rose and picked up a bundle, and his wife trailed after him, carrying the infant. They left the train, which continued to shake and rock as it moved away from the feeble light that trembled in the gloom. Following the singer's departure, silence reigned until a beggar at the end of the carriage announced, "That was Khudayri himself."

I looked out the window; the night was scattering its stars like silver liras over the dark, silent desert expanses. Here a question burst forth, cascading like rays from a silver star: Do the earth's cities create their trains, or do the mobile train-cities create their stations and stationary cities?

Friday's Gifts

The Night Beggar

FRIDAY IS BOTH the memory of a name and the name of a memory. It is the repository of all that day's gifts and that night's secrets, because Friday is the day's answer to the night's question. It is free circulation and a preordained gathering. It is people, selection, mutual recognition, rising, assembly, and the straight path. My memories of Friday include the house's flat roof, eating outdoors there, the family dinner on the roof beneath a see-sawing heaven where shooting stars fell like a flaming tongue dangling from the toothless mouth of primordial substance, a child's bed flying through the dark and colliding with tremulous stars, the railings, television antennae, jugs of water, and dovecotes. You could hear the mosquito nets' susurration, trickling secretions, and unexpected noises from the street.

Once the day ended, the night beggar arrived. He was a mendicant who collected scraps from dinner, leftovers from families who had bolted their doors with the setting of the sun. Friday for this beggar meant light for his eyes and warmth for his feet; not to mention leftover rice, bread, and fruit. We would know he was passing down the alley when we heard his stick tap the ground and his appeal break through the doors' silence. We never saw him, and it was his voice that reminded us of the existence of this blind skeleton who plunged into the darkness from one Friday to the next. Entirely on his own, he recognized the different doors and slowed his pace a bit in front of each. He could see with his heart, whereas we were blind in our imaginations. We pictured him as a semi-material being, who was in some sense preternatural and who filled his bag with everything we did not understand. He was a questioning plea that lingered overnight outside our houses. If your household turned you out, you would become a mendicant; you would turn into a beggar in the alley of great gifts.

I remember a beggar who was considered a guest in our home. He had a dark brown face and was bleary-eyed. His nose was runny, his sandals patched, and the ropes for his red head-cloth were dusty. You smelled the age of his coat even before he approached the dinner table . . . that crazy old man. He was the first beggar I saw. I was told he was a forgotten relative of ours. From then on, because I never saw another night beggar besides him, I have reconciled myself to the idea that every family has a relative who is crazy or a wandering mendicant. People who write short stories all have relatives who are crazy or beggars. For an author, every day is Friday. If writers lack such kin, they themselves become beggars and the stories are the gifts.

The Day Beggar

When the night beggar vanishes, he is replaced by the day beggar, who then begins to practice his trade. The day beggar is not a solitary soul but part of a group, and the phrase referring to him implies as much. He will be found at his ease in a coffee shop, washing himself at a public bath, seated in the barber's chair, squeezing into a crowded market, an invited guest at a banquet, watching a movie at the cinema, and praying at a mosque. He is traceable by name, description, appearance, and number. The day beggar is not excluded from the boon termed communal solidarity. (Those condemned by society to solitude find that Friday—the day of worshipful gathering—is just another nameless day, because they have been barred—secluded within their walls—from Friday's gifts, which are implied by the day's Arabic name, which refers to collective sanctity. When you are excluded from participating in Friday, you are cursed and banished. This condition is experienced only by those isolated from their families in sickbeds or behind bars.)

By breaking down the walls that shelter customs, we learn about these customs and their role. Then each of us will observe his fingers when they reach for a set of prayer beads, rub or finger them, tug at a mustache, scratch, grasp, or poke. We lean down to tie a shoe lace or turn toward mirrors when counting money. Ever since light first caressed us, our shriek of surprise has continued to grow as we are confronted by machinery that directs, compromises, and chains us to the mechanism that resembles a waterwheel, with its muffled squeal. Break the chain to isolate yourself and thus become an alien among faces—oblivious to the communal party of getting to know each other. Cutting the chain separates you from the answer and distances you from a week of customs, from transformative legend. The question, however, stretches out, beginning at the legend's base, beyond the city, beginning in times before the coffee-house, bath, restaurant, barber shop, and cinema.

Our legends oppress our hearts and stand guard over our lips, which have tired of stories about swampy lakes, skiffs, fishing, planting, harvesting, hunting, emigration, and murder. The most famous of these is the merry legend about the long trip to the city, about roaming through the souks, going inside a restaurant, prayer in the mosque, and then a return to the village with news.

The legend begins with an evening gathering in the guesthouse to bid farewell to a tribesman who will leave for the city on Friday morning. The group casts anxious, envious, and hopeful looks at the happy man. Meanwhile the breathing and yawning of their mouths act like bellows for the coals resting beneath reed bundles on the hearth, the lantern's trembling flame, and the looks of champions of the communal spirit who brandish split-blade swords or long rifles. The merry legend travels in company with the gnats, men's head-ropes, colored wool carpets, thin rolled cigarettes, coffee jugs, and brown faces molded from river clay, the guts of slain fathers, sperm cells journeying through the wombs of combative, stalwart women, the original grandmothers, mothers with green-tinged tattoos of crosses and beads, and the happy young women educated in schools floating on reed islands. Toward the end of the evening, when fatigue has bested men wrestling with an urge to depart, the chosen man lags behind with the village's totem, which has slipped out of the large coffeepot resting on the hearth. Together, the next morning, the two will follow exceptionally rugged roads toward the distant city.

The villager, his back stooped, watches the waiter place dishes on the table in front of him. Sturdy fingers busily manipulate bits of bread soaked in broth. Through the aroma of roast meat, pickles, and onion, the absent family members join the father in consuming the tasty meal as if with a single mouth. On the table, which gleams with the sun's rays that penetrate the establishment's front window, the father has ranged the spirits of his dogs, cats, chickens, wife, and children—cheek by jowl with the hungry specter of his totem—so that each can participate in this leisurely repast. The restaurant is vast—greater than all the troughs in the village. It seems even larger on account of the mirrors, in which the villager observes his companions at tables, no matter where his eyes roam. Everyone is licking bones, fingers, or lips. So the villager whispers to himself, as he burps and looks at the restaurant's pictures, mirrors, and waiters, who are scurrying between the tables, "I've eaten for all of you."

Social activists and literature teachers have forgotten this last villager lost in the crush of Friday's markets. The disappearance from the Iraqi short story of the last exemplar of the country bumpkin in the city has meant the related disappearance of the first hawker from the peddler's flea market, the porter from the merchants' caravansaries, the masseur from the public bath, and the cotton carder. The first migrants settled in the city, and their children adopted new professions—in the souks of the perfume vendors, coppersmiths, moneychangers, carpenters, goldsmiths, clock makers, and potters. Some also mastered the Indians' secret of mixing spices.

Before I wash my hands of the villager, I will recall the original appearance of the used-clothing souk, which was connected to the peddler's market. Manchester wool overcoats with large buttons, tweed jackets with distinctive leather elbow patches, waterproof raingear, white Arrow-brand shirts, and gray serge trousers hung on a long, depressing façade. These clothes were sent to laundries to rid them of spots acquired through neglect and transfer from body to body, from one set of circumstances to another, and from one address to the subsequent one. Hems brushed the heads of people passing beneath the long façade of garments. New bodies shuddered

133

at the mysterious feel of the life of the previous owners, because the benzene scent of spot removers had not totally eradicated it. I do not know the number of villagers whom the city will captivate with its overcoats while I tell the following story.

The dream of the messenger in the rural school where I taught was to acquire an overcoat from that souk. The day I presented him with an overcoat I had purchased for only a few dirhams, he lost his normal composure. The good-hearted pilgrim became a man who—clad in his heavy, black English overcoat and looking like a resident alien—entered the village guesthouse, which was crowded with farmers clad in light cloaks. It was a symbol of enlightenment—one of many—that visited the distant village occasionally, bearing various names. I do not know what became of this pilgrim, from whom I have been separated for many years. I may have been reminded of him by a boy selling tea by night in the train station. All those new vendors in the Friday markets emerged, so to speak, from the overcoats of that souk.

The city awakens to a single cry in a shared, open space that weekday markets have vacated for the Friday one. This souk is the outgrowth of all the others but lacks classifications, price structure, and controls for weights and measures. Used goods are arranged in topsy-turvy fashion in a festival for odds and ends. I visit the Friday market to assure myself of the existence of a certain specimen I expect to find among those loitering in the souk. I want to see him in the flesh. At the close of the day I will follow him to the small museum of inconsequential items he has accumulated during circuits of the souk. He actually exists. I can draw his portrait; he is surrounded by useless items. The museum contains all the bric-a-brac you have seen and some you have not:

a long, bronze key (with the teeth cut to open the bolt of a lock as if with the letters of a secret password—thus sending you the echo of a door closing slowly on the bones of the past, pulverizing them), a mouse trap that disturbed me for nights, reminding me of the timeworn story of the piper who tempted a troupe of mice to their destruction in a river with the melodies of his mizmar, a small grindstone, a dagger, scissors, an inkwell, a needle for binding books, a kohl applicator, pins, coins, and dead and bygone things without any use in normal life today. The trivia collector stretches out on his bed, fixing his gaze on the chandelier that hangs from the ceiling. Dangling from it are crystal serpents in whose heads are set glassy stones for a poisoned, multicolored dream. Like me, he dreams of a huge, mouse-devouring contraption that consumes in one gulp an entire troupe of mice. It consists of a netted cage, three meters long and wide, and half a meter high. Retractable springs hidden deep inside the cage connect to side bars that support the raised door. The least pressure on the springs will cause the bars to retract, thus allowing the door to fall instantly, trapping the troupe of mice inside. Then the mice are at the mercy of a lethal, spiked, iron plate, the same size as the roof of the giant trap. Once the door has fallen, trapping the mice, the plate is lowered automatically, lacerating their stunned bodies with its multiple, pointed spikes.

I have read about machines like this in the stories "The Pit and the Pendulum" by Edgar Allan Poe and "In the Penal Colony" by Franz Kafka. I do not know what inspired those authors with their disturbing ideas. I am certain, however, that authors who portray grand realities do not wander far from an area that features museums for inane items gleaned from Friday markets.

The Hammam of Happiness

Feeling stripped, liberated, at peace, and melded are sequels to the first step in the process of public bathing. Along with his clothes, the bather sheds all his associations in the changing room. He strips off his transitory identity to dissolve in a steamy area that denies any personal identification. The chambers in a public bath have been designed to correspond to the way-stations of a quest for personal dissolution and annihilation in the final white basin of the Unknown, after the body has been reduced through the extraordinary process of being progressively stripped ever barer, like a sugar cube.

The public bath I frequent is in a roofed area centrally located at the hub of the souks. The low doorway is masked by a curtain. I descend to the warm changing room—oleander flowers, cotton boll, and stick cinnamon*—and proceed to the benches that are spread with waist wraps and wet towels. When I leave the changing room and pull back the sweat room's curtain, I find myself surrounded by naked friends, sons of the bridges. We are amazed to meet like this: so naked, so similar. Then we all advance to the chamber where our bodies dissolve amid assorted complaints while we spread out among pillars of steam and the heat distends our sexual organs. We release our complaints about imaginary pains, aging, fatigue, subjugation— along with the dirt. Slowly moving hands remove particles of dirt, hair, and dead skin. In the recovery chamber, our bodies return to

---

* Figurative expressions for succumbing to the changing room. (A)

us. Some of us are flabby with smooth skins and limbs, and some display warts, tattoos, prominent belly buttons, and scars. Some bodies overflow the human norm, whereas others self-confidently adhere to it. A third group's eyes keep returning to their scrawny physiques. These are waxy, shadowless bodies, statues with bent backs and only a vaporous existence. Then we settle in the central hall beneath the bath's recessed, ribbed dome, as daylight flows from its lofty windows. Steam condenses inside and changes to droplets of warm water that leave us semi-conscious, as we slip ever deeper into daydreams and grow ever less involved with the world around us. This is the "fabricating" chamber, where I met the liar. He told such huge lies that he turned into a penis that wriggled across the baths' tiles, leaping from basin to basin, until he finally dissolved in a steam cloud among feathers of daylight that fell in fragments from the dome. This man exists only in the public baths—along with the laughing man, the weeping man, and the sarcastic man. These are all bath mutants—viperous men. After three empty chambers, our bodies unite into a single naked form that sinks into a large basin beneath a hot rain that awakens in our veins the pleasure of seclusion and liberation from bodily fetters. There we find a desert-like lethargy, a cottony numbness, motionless artificial trees, a pale sun, and a shiny marble floor. In the distance, spewing perfumed vapors, looms a huge sphere like the egg of Sindbad's roc. White doves land on the basin's edge and change into girls, who plunge into the water. Their slender bodies and bantam feet are mirrored by the marble. Then they undergo a metamorphosis to become birds and take flight. Behind the sphere, a white ship appears and glides across the marble floor. It snatches the shape-shifting birds and then disappears in the steam's whistling whirlpools, leaving behind a pervasive whiteness.

Perfumed drops of rain fall while invisible anklets jingle. From the steam flow red mouths that suck on the unitary body. For bathers, the return through the various chambers and basins seems a repeated dream in which they recall all the establishment's chambers, basins, benches, and curtains. There is no set path to follow; they suddenly find themselves in the changing room, where they reclaim their clothes and exit via the bath's curtain.

A Seat in the Dark

A stack of old cinema posters for films from Twentieth Century Fox, Hollywood, Universal, and from Egyptian films of the mid-twentieth century carried me back to all the times I sat limp in a seat in the dark, facing the wall screen and the Technicolor manifestations on my adolescent sensibility of the first 3-D film shown in the summer movie house. That film was *The Robe*, which starred Victor Mature, Richard Burton, and Jean Simmons. The posters also reminded me of showings, morning and evening, of a series of films: *Robin Hood*, *Broken Lance*, starring Spencer Tracy, *The Sword in the Stone*, which was a Disney production, *Ali Baba and the Forty Thieves*, and *The Thief of Baghdad*. I remember a morning viewing of the film *The Egyptian* in the winter cinema (al-Rashid) toward the end of 1955.

It is ten o'clock. The adolescent with a thin, brown face, full lips, and a faint mustache, wearing baggy, wide pants, bids daylight adieu and strolls into the gallery of seats that are supervised and crowded, in the lower area, the location for seats costing only forty fils. He takes his place among shoulders, knees, and eyes. He has allocated to his hunger a hardboiled egg wrapped in pita bread, which he purchased from a food cart stationed at the cinema's entry. He consumes it with a cup of spiced mango pickles (amba) while he waits for the color rays to flow from a dark aperture and transport him to the planet of the movies.

The lights in the hall are gradually extinguished. The warning whistle blows. Pleat by pleat the curtain in front of the screen disappears. Then here is the picture of the king and the flag. Next are previews of coming attractions, an edition of news of the world in pictures, and the cartoons. During an intermission before the feature, the young man visits the restroom, returning to his seat in the row of viewers in response to the warning bell's unique ring. In a grandiose, legendary production, history is unfurled before his eyes. A struggle flares within golden decors and the masks of pharaonic faces. The curtain opens to reveal his future with real-life struggles around his Iraqi hut. There are dialogues, action scenes, and sexual situations that will influence the destiny of his impoverished imagination. A crimson fever inflames his eyelids, and screen music chokes his throat while he watches the Red Indians' horses. Throbs of love and its songs set fire to his lungs, and the blazing Roman cities singe his ribs. The props of the Friday morning films were the lance, rifle, revolver, cannon, a tunic studded with gems, magic carpets, and volcanoes. The settings were jungles along the Amazon and Mississippi rivers, the world's deserts, pirate ships, and the pyramids. The characters were mutants, gorillas, steers, Amazon warriors, gangs, clowns, and beautiful women. After all this, the adolescent is tossed back to the blinding light of day and to the predictably barbaric weather conditions outside the cinema. From one Friday to the next, posters for the films parade along al-Ashar Street on a big board carried on the shoulders of boys who work for the movie theater. They are preceded by a clown from the advertisements (as in *Tuman the Piper*) or line up along the bridge's railing for *River of No Return* as dazzled crowds pass by. Dreary streets borrow from these pictures on the move their gaudy colors. The subjugated populace compensate for their humiliating defeats with these counterfeit heroics. A personality undermined by defeat and self-reflexive disappointment connives to steal through the gaps of lost worlds into the bedchambers of royal palaces. We are involuntary members of a gang *(Robin Hood)* in an imaginary forest near castles rife with pleasures, intrigues, and wars—a possible retreat and an acceptable form of escape, hiding out (until the promised day) in a happy land where the barriers between fantasy and reality fade.

That was the experience derived from the cinematic climate at the middle of the twentieth century before it was marred by the acute agitation of the chair in the dark. The scandalous acts of sex films awakened the lust of the cinema audience to shameless displays and stealthy glances at the mysterious mechanics of love. Film portrayed sexual intercourse as a remote practice and a nearly impossible relationship that a viewer watched and discussed, reacting to it and narrating it. With the passing days, the influence of the film changed. It became the viewer's personal serial that played in a lustrous gloom. His hunger for any leg, thigh, face, voice, signal, and wink became excruciating. The female sexual performer—stripped of any dramatic importance—became a naked symbol dis-associated from the actors who excelled in portraying her on the screen. After a simulated kiss—to express love interest tied to the events of the film—had aroused a profound, sensual contentment, the audience members were not satisfied with ten stimulating nude scenes to calm each youth's appetite for personal, sexual subjugation. The upshot was a sexual climate that was somewhat secret, stinging, and repressive; how can we describe this atmosphere?

An eye-opening film, in which actresses remove their clothing as easily as they have a bite to eat, lasts only a couple of hours, whereas the viewer is left with twenty-two hours of anxiety, while he is supervised and subjected to ruthless social pressure. He devises methods involving substitution and self-destructive behavior, which only increase his repression, thirst, and daydreams. Thus the gap widens between viewing and acting, between image and body, and between the symbol and the original it represents. Those who make the ignominious video exploit the confusions of our emotional life to shred our equilibrium, which our defense of the hymen has preserved for us. These films terminate our masculine virginity and transform each member of the audience into a voyeur who buys for the price of a cheap ticket the right to a secret excursion, which begins in the first room in the street next to the cinema. The theater is totally dark (although this is not required for an individual video), and the darkness does not merely hide our reactions but also rises like an impregnable privacy shield to surround the individual's chair during his excursion, flirtations, and dalliance with his long-haired beast. He would trip over the furniture in the film and ignore the sequence of events in it in order to reach the pure nudity suspended in the curtain of light above his head. The viewer becomes experienced at substituting for the disjointed plot of the film exculpatory ones fabricated by his imagination. The film is his alone. What he views is presented solely for his sake. He is the master of the cinema, the actors, and all his surroundings. He possesses a Sodom, which has disappeared definitively from his world. Then he regains consciousness in his chair and slips out, feeling abandoned.

It was an oppressive phase, those secret visits to ignoble cinemas, before we finally regained our equilibrium in a journey of the imagination, because the image borrowed from outside our walls was unable to satisfy our need to depict our changing world. Our progress must proceed through our own tribulations and our lives' roles. All the same, we still view a new film with our trained sensibility, which chooses from the roles what will fit the old image, harking back to that distant morning when we watched the Friday film: the film that haggled for our innocence, gaining the upper hand over us in the dark, but losing ground to us in the daylight.

House of Names

A meter reader told me about a house in Old Basra. It was one of the houses linked to the fish and vegetable markets. These are near the cart stop, a rest area for cab drivers, and appliance repairmen. When he entered it, he would find—the door was open all day long—at the side of the vestibule a door with 'toilet' written on it in chalk. Opposite that was another door on which was written, in chalk as well, "door to stairs." The meter reader did not need to reach the house's courtyard, which was open to the sky and paved with broad, baked bricks, because the water meter was beneath the stairs in a small wooden box on which was written "water meter." Above this was an "electric meter" box. A flood of daylight disclosed other inscriptions designating the closed doors opening onto the courtyard. These were labeled: "Alawiya's room," "Granny Karima's room," "Salih's room," "Marhun's room," "the bride's room," "bath," and "kitchen." The strangest of these inscriptions was that on the door of the "lame people's room." A child had practiced his writing by naming the things in his house and the rooms with crude, unsteady chalk marks in exactly the same way he would name items in a picture he drew in his school sketchbook. So, here is "a fish," "a river," "a woman," or "a car." (When he makes a spelling mistake, pictures from his boyish fantasies and images from writing exercises slip into the items he has named.) Thus he has tried to keep his family's house from being deserted, sad, and silent when the family members leave it. Although on the days he entered it, the meter reader never encountered any hunchbacked beast or human being coming out of "Alawiya's room" or an irascible person bursting out of "Marhun's room," he still feels that these inscriptions are indicative of the presence of residents and of the suppressed commotion of life occurring behind the doors in that house with its doors wide open. In the same way, in the rusty trash can, set unceremoniously by a house's entry, are interred heaps of the previous evening's fabrications, wrapped up with the leftovers from banquets held inside.

As if in a story, one room in the house was left without a name to designate its contents, leaving it instead a room with hot secrets. In it was born the future child, the writer of the names. Let us descend the steps to a room where a woman is giving birth, assisted by three other women who are gathered on a wide mattress near a stove. The sleepless women are skilled in conversation, jesting, and supplication. The expectant mother does not participate in their collective preparations for her delivery or their talk about labor pains, relaxation, the promise of family life, and the joys of nursing. She resists the medicinal smells and the vapors rising from the basin, the powder, and the clean, white sheets. The light falling from the light fixture in the room rocks like a knife hanging from a thin thread that never snaps. The expectant mother pants in time to the contractions of her uterus as these lift her like white wings over the swamp of plasma and antiseptics, over the tongs and the scissors. A sharp cry ends this banquet with the arrival of a live lump of flesh, as Friday's child is born. Years later the child will write on the nameless room where he was born a name that grew in his belly button. He will label it "the honey room," for no obvious reason, unless it was a misspelling or a childish confusion about the name of his mother, whose identity has been lost in the shadows of the house of names.

Morning Airs and Nocturnes
A War Diary

We go to war; then we reach birth.
Mahmud Darwish

The Tenth Nocturne

THE NIGHT WAS spattered with thousands of artillery rounds and the sirens of speeding ambulances. The night shook with thousands of explosions, whereas the earth was stable enough for the tongue of death to loll over it, licking away at the city's body. Walls, doors, windows, and roofs rocked, and this night was dreadfully dark. The night was covered by a million cloaks and blankets, a rifle, a rib, an eye. This night's teeth clacked together, and it raged, terrifyingly black. In a continuous growl, locks were crushed and glass shattered. With anxiety and compassion the mothers let their cloaks hang down to cover the great heart of the city, holding out their hands to enclose and protect it. A million sleepless hearts, thumps that continued in rapid succession, competing with each other, even and odd numbers, a roar and a fading away, a sobbing and a declamation, fear and prayer. Then these were organized and harmonized into a single rhythm: a beat, a beat in a gracious evening that cloaked the terrifying lament for a tattered night with disheveled hair, so that it quieted down, became calm, and softly hummed a familiar tune that traveled from house to house until it reached the soldiers in the trenches beyond the river.

My heart feels calmer, and my hand moves from the book to the radio and then back to the book. It is five a.m., dawn, and the tenth night since the last attack began. In my head there is a map of the city: each street, house, coffee shop, date palm, river, oar, and sail to the south, along with the familiar faces of my friends. Kazim al-Hajjaj calls to tell me that a bomb fell on Mahmud Abd al-Wahhab's house but that he was not home, praise God. Warid al-Salim calls and says that Jawad al-Hattab and Muhammad Shakir al-Sab' set out in the morning for the front and still have not returned. Don't worry . . . we have a right to worry. What about the others? Al-Barikan, al-Zahir, al-Tamimi, al-Jarrakh, al-Ahmadi, al-Rabbat, al-Sa'idi, al-Badr, al-Mu'aybad, al-Bazi, al-Basri, Husayn, Abd al-Khaliq, Salman, Faruq, Hatim, Mahdi, Majid, Qasim, Jamil, Abd al-Samad, and Khalil . . . there are many of us, by God. Where are the others? I personally confided all of them to the safekeeping of this perforated night, in which no hole was sealed without another breaking open. I swear by the ten nights. This nation has endured; so do not worry. Dawn will seal all the holes. I swear by the dawn. How strange this is! My hand, while trying to stem the radio's tide, stumbles upon a familiar tune: a Nocturne by Chopin. Unknown but sympathetic fingers perform on the ether's piano this major piece, and its sweet reverberation caresses sleepless eyes with dawn's delicate fingers. The world is alive. The nation is alive. We are alive.

Along the Eastern Street

A warm morning . . . another sunrise to a war-torn morning air. There is intermittent bombardment, but my adventuresome guardian angel tempts me out of the house on an excursion. You have a great need to mix with groups of the people who remain in the city! There in the markets and coffeehouses, in outlying areas! I make my way along the side of the wide, asphalt street. There are few vehicles and even fewer pedestrians. Indeed, no one else is out walking; an empty street is flooded by the warm sun. The recent rains have created a vast pool on each side. From the front, there is a faint grumble that the steadfast walls of a group of modern homes absorb. Except for that, there is a deep silence. I pay careful attention to my footing and to the sound of my shoes on the asphalt. A twisting garden path springs to mind. It is a still, empty lane, but a dog leaps into a curve from an opening in the mud-brick wall that runs beside the lane and then enters a hole in the opposite wall. Then the lane is empty. It cuts through the orchard, twisting endlessly in the midst of an all-embracing, natural silence. You take a step, descend to the street, alone. (Keep a lid on your imagination.) There is a real street and a clear sky against which the high silver wings of warplanes stand out. They leave behind a roar that fades into the deep blue. I pass a group of Egyptian workers on a scaffold. I greet them and they return the greeting with beaming enthusiasm. There is a mutual understanding; defense of the homeland is a right, and death is a right, but work is also a right. Spare yourself deep thoughts. Stay on the surface. Here are work's realities beside you. Here is its refuse: scrap metal, used motors, and empty oil cans. On the flood water, there is a flock of gulls that the tumult of nearby artillery fire has driven from the bank of the river to this pool. Suddenly my steps halt. A violent sound sucks my breath away and plunges me into the wall of blind emptiness. On the far side of the pool, a shell has fallen. The surprise was not total, for my steps stopped when I heard the shriek of the incoming projectile. After the explosion's reverberation, the flock of birds rises in a single white clump, soaring over the pool, but the explosion has frozen me where I stood. The flock did not soar until it had digested this powerful shockwave. The birds were perplexed by this sudden jolt of sound in nature's spacious bird cage. They did not land again on the pool's surface until the earth, houses, and water had imbibed the explosion's draft, the smell of gunpowder had dissipated, and the breeze had swept away the smoke. The flock's descent after numerous circles in the air was like a fleeting dream and sprang forth the way the dirt lane through the orchards had sprung to mind. I recalled quite clearly the image of the white wings as they rose, the calm circling, and then the slow settling on the water, time and again, before it could vanish into my head with the preceding dream. Just as the vision of the rural lane had renewed my ability to move prior to the explosion, scattered impressions of the flock immediately calmed my soul and allowed my feet to fall beside the road with quiet confidence: a road that does not end, and dreams the war creates and archives in our living memories.

Glass Nocturne

The traitorous glass remains cheerful. How treacherous it is! It keeps falling, smashing, and shattering with every shock wave from a deceitful bomb or quake following a round of fire from our artillery positions scattered throughout the city or even when a plane breaks the sound barrier. It remains cheerful, not distinguishing between enemy or friend, between one gun and another. Our ears, which have grown accustomed to the inferno's hymns, can distinguish tonight between the muffled sound of a tank gun, the combined retreat of heavy artillery, the storm of missiles, and the exploding blast of shells. Glass, however, shakes, submits to any pressure, and breaks, whether in house windows, coffeehouses, warehouses, vehicles, mirrors, glass tumblers, inkwells, vases, pictures, dolls, clocks, or spectacles. You should certainly never trust glass anymore. I gaze at a large window reinforced with crisscrossed strips of tape and remember the earth traversed by the tracks of armored vehicles, which leave furrows and many deep, intersecting ruts. The grass-covered earth has been scarred by bombs and sectioned off by trenches. The pitted green plains, decapitated date palms, and bloodied waterwheels notwithstanding, this earth will soon recapture its natural quality, resume its course, and master the future of its soil. This glass, however, throws itself into the void, leaving its splinters to describe a short, sad trajectory. This glass will never help improve our vision, which wants to see ever farther. It will never allow our images to transit it silently, safely, and steadfastly to the flowery fields of our dreams.

Contact with life's living skin and my apprehension, passion, and instinct have goaded me to replace this glass with plexiglass made with silicone. Flakes and tendrils of ultimate clarity and strength insert you into your surroundings outside and perhaps even inside. When you look, you are not conscious of any barrier or distortion. It allows a truthful, direct, authoritative vision of the distant essence—which is latent and authentic—and of the heart of the flame, which subdues the earth and purifies it of evils.

The Only Choice

I go out to the markets, since they are a place that links us to the reality of this historic city more truly than any other location. There I slip in among the people. (There is nothing warmer or more precious than this word "people.") The congestion in the souk, in these days of war, is pleasant. There is an intimate impression of the warm spirit that unites everyone, the inhabitants of the city's center and those who come from its outskirts: soldiers, women, and loiterers. At the center of this clamor, in which there are no quarrels or disagreements over prices and no crowding around merchandise, your glance falls on a man the war has disabled: someone with a crutch or in a wheelchair, with amputated limbs and empty sleeves, which hang down or are crammed into pockets. One quickly senses the shared feeling that envelops this man when he passes in front of a coffeehouse, pauses at a stop for shared-ride vehicles, or joins others in their daily festival of selling and buying. We need people like him in order to keep the city moving, for this market to continue, and to combat others bravely. We cannot keep ourselves, however, from also pursuing another oppressive feeling—that of not measuring up, since none of us was granted this man's opportunity to lose a limb in a real battle. We still enjoy our health and are able-bodied. As soon as our eyes meet, his fleeting glance discloses the only choice, the necessary choice, to which the poet Mikhail Lukonin referred:

> *In that stormy reverberation*
> *The choices were limited;*
> *And returning with an empty sleeve*
> *Was preferable to returning*
> *With an empty spirit.*

Familiar Serpents

I maintain a small archive for wars: a small notebook in which I stick pictures cut from newspapers published during the Arab wars of 1967 and 1973, and the Lebanese Civil War. When I take it out to flip through the faded images, two photos catch my eye. The first, from the June War, is of an aged man who stands beside an unexploded bomb, which is much taller than he is and which sticks into the ground on its tapered end. The old man embraces the bomb with both his scrawny hands, and his face is etched with incredulity and anxiety. The second photograph, from the October War, portrays a hyena-like animal sticking out its tail and opening its jaws as wide as possible to look terrifying. Confronting it is a tank. These two protagonists are surrounded by the Sinai's vast sands. Beneath this photo is the caption, "Strange Encounter in the Desert."

The encounter between wild animals and men with weapons is repeated in every war. There is nothing strange about an encounter like this, where the roar of tanks mingles with that of wild beasts. In their stubborn confrontation, a common bond unites them in a single ditch with a single goal: to shred the enemy with fangs, claws, and bows. The man, however, is amazed by another, opposite state: the wild beast's respect for the corpse tossed on sacred ground. It approaches the body, sniffs and toys with it, but shuns its blood and flesh. Moreover, the unknown nature of the corpse makes it equivalent in status for this beast with other corpses by which it will squat with snow-white teeth. Snakes may seek the shade provided by soldiers' damp dugouts and hide between sand bags, wooden posts, and sheet metal. When the earth shakes from a shell, the snake dangles down over the soldiers from the dugout's ceiling. Then it twists back up and returns to its secure nook, oblivious to the human glances, faces, or breathing beneath it. Their association lasts a long time. During lengthy evenings, soldiers swap stories and news, knowing that their neighbor is overhead. In the narrator's mind lurks the idea that a legend from bygone days will transform this snake into a sentient being that understands and requests more details, relishing the tale. That was our own special legend. Our own compassionate land sends its dumb creatures to lighten the impact on soldiers of the night, their watch, and their confused feelings. It decreases the desolation of their situation by sharing their daily bread, serving as a charm for their courage, and granting them the memory of a friendship with a familiar creature, even if it is a snake.

I Should Erase and Draw

Three of us were together when someone suggested that we should explore the other part of the city: the dangerous area near the Shatt al-Arab. Abbas' car (his Volkswagen that was demolished a few days later by a bomb) shot off with us smoothly and gracefully. Its speed continued to increase on the empty street, for it was propelled by the force of the warm steel and the constant muffled roar of the exhaust, although we sensed only an indistinct, submerged call issuing from the day and enticing our vehicle toward it, as if beckoning an inquisitive, throbbing spirit. Mahmud sat beside Abbas, and from the back seat I observed the speedometer respond to that appeal. We were cruising along at a hundred kilometers an hour, and the car was like a large eraser, rubbing out all the scenery around it. The cleared space pushed other scenes toward us, but the car quickly erased those in turn. We crossed the Ashar River, and signs for places we knew began to whiz past. We did not notice until after our fleeting passage, when we were beyond them, that their large, glass façades were smashed. They were different now. Their forms were new. Signboards were askew and doors were torn away. (I should erase and draw: erase a restaurant and draw a burned-out structure. I should erase a cinema and draw an abandoned building. I should erase a coffeehouse and draw a closed business.) The speeding car swung toward the Corniche along the river. We were astonished by the calm mood of the river. Our eyes noticed the motion of white wings coming together, separating, and then flying off toward the smooth water surface. There we found a long line of fortifications, a string of helmets, distant ships, and the roots of flourishing trees. (In days, a bomb will uproot a tree, and a boat anchored there will plant another.) Abbas may have increased the speed, for the car was sailing over the river. We caught sight of dozens of wooden boats laden with dates. The winds were guiding them toward the Gulf in a dreamy vision created by dancing molecules of gleaming, still water. (I should erase and draw. I erase a boy swimming and draw a soldier. I should erase a fishing pole and draw a rifle. I should erase a skiff and pencil in a military bridge. I should erase embarrassment and hesitation and draw instead manliness and daring.) We returned from our little adventure after a few more scouting patrols at the same speed down the empty streets of al-Ashar. I looked at the two faces in the front seat and surmised the thoughts and projects that were percolating beneath their faces' rough skins. Each of us was concocting his own stew: what he would erase and draw. He should erase an old coffeehouse and build a new one in that spot. He should sweep up all the shattered glass and install a new façade. How quickly everything will rise again! Steps will continue to traverse streets the length and breadth of the city. We should erase a river and draw one with a lighthouse that will glow like a green eye that does not slumber. We should erase a city and build a paradise.

Alphabet Juice

I read the following paragraph in a story by the Czech author Jiri Marek.

War flared up, and this did not mean anything special, because we all were seared by its fire. We know very well what the word "war" means. It is precisely a word composed of three letters. It is, however, not an exceptionally appropriate word for war, since it seems to me to be quite a soft word. "War" ought rather to be a word that devastates and hurts. The smoke of gunfire ought to emerge from it. It ought to freeze the blood in our veins. . . . This word "war" remains nothing when compared to the real thing.

We know that words do not suffice, although each tongue has its own fields, seasons, climates, and trees that produce letters with a special juice. We do not merely read the word; before us appears a ripe fruit that intoxicates and soars away with us. Thus we also ponder the Arabic word for war: *harb*. I do not know of a word closer to it than *hubb* (love), and its letters epitomize the flame of life precisely and steadfastly. In our seasons, we know of no other two trees like these flourishing ones from the Arabic family . . . the longest-lived and most profusely useful. Their fruits are distinguished by one consonant. The *harb* tree conceals among its branches fright, annihilation, and separation. The *hubb* tree offers beauty, jealousy, and union. These two words are two trees sprouting in a changeable desert climate, in a field scarred by horses' hooves, pulsing and ablaze with virginal red flowers, the touch of which suffices to fell recalcitrant Tatar hearts. In the belly of this field are buried the skulls of Sultan Murad, the British conqueror Maude, the warrior Hulegu, and bronze boxes inside which were tightly sealed the hearts of Istar, Layla, Buthayna, and other female martyrs of passion, whether during periods of occupation, slavery, and unrest or in times of cultural flowering, freedom, and stability.

It is more than a linguistic coincidence that the Arabic word *radan* (destruction) originates with the letter that *hubb* lacks for it to become *harb*. Why should it be surprising that the Arabic word *hayat* (life) begins with the letter that also starts the opposite word *hatf* (death) and at the same time concludes the list of the four previous words, which are the coldest, most infernal, and punishing nouns all at the same time.

With the same simplicity and spontaneity with which we transpose or add letters to these words, we can shuffle the consonants of the word *harb* to make *hibr* (ink). Thus we discover the secret of metaphorical correlation in a catchphrase like: he wrote his short story (or poem) in letters of his own blood.

I believe that inspirations like these, drawing on memory, etymology, and the appearance of words written on the page, will exert a special and profound influence on consonantal studies in Arabic. Then, with the same blend and procedure, more than one consonant will be shared by four contradictory words like *qasf* (bombardment) and *qans* (hunting)—which refer to death and war—and *raqs* (dance) and *wasala* (arrive)—which refer to life and love.

When we need a fifth word to close the circle of the four previous ones, let us turn to the word *qassa* (narrate), with its widespread possibilities of rounding up and recounting the realities of the war and the events of life in all colors from pitch black to luminous. What appears to be a simple meditation on the word *harb* (war) via the game of shared letters seems to be more than that after a study of consonantal concentration. It is a deeper linguistic study in a text with direct bearing on the reality of war, to which Jiri Marek pointed in the paragraph above.

We will produce comparable results but in a different sequence. All the consonants will participate in isolating the essential juice of each, for more than one tree in our extensive field.

Moons and String Instruments

I hear the same tune repeated on the city's empty streets. It is echoed by the damp, wooden balconies, the girders of bridges (the rustic bridge over a grassy creek is one of them), and the metal posts with holes in them. You all will see that these are merely dream symbols, photographic images that evolve in an album of the five musicians who performed in an Eastern music ensemble in an apartment with a wooden balcony. (I make my way with difficulty among my symbols.) The roads are empty, the darkness is drunken, and the lights from distant balconies at the crossroads are flickering, thus establishing forlorn distances for things. Then they inspire monsters that change persistently like those creeping metal creatures in the avant-garde film *Marsighan*. All the same, it truly is a quiet night. The artillery is holding off playing its customary march of saxophones with 175-millimeter mouthpieces.

It was late when I left the house, after midnight or toward dawn. I traversed the deserted park and passed by poles that once supported streetlights. The breeze passing through them caused the holes to emit an intermittent or continuous whistling. (That was when musical lampposts entered the desert of Basrayatha.) I was approaching my goal. I crossed a bridge and traversed the ancient souk. Signs from demolished shops dangled over the souk's passageway. The close-set wooden balconies, stamped with the insignia of tradesmen, money-changers, pharmacists, physicians, and spice dealers, dripped with water. Their doors were open and the stairways dark. The wood was scraped and peeling. The silence was dense. (I could still hear the melody.) I reached a vestibule into which the moon shone. The wood of the balconies was laughing from teeth that smoke had damaged. These were tinted the same yellow as the damp brick story bracketed between the signboards.

I climbed the stairs, opened the apartment door with an antique key, laughed out loud in the face of the five musicians, and called out, "Softly, softly; you know how dangerous it is. So I deserve three pieces at least. What will I hear first? Music for lovers? Musical recollections of youth? Fine . . . I'll be satisfied with a medley from Iraq's musical heritage. You know how dangerous it is. There may not be another peaceful moonlit night. What? I perceive the fingers' awkwardness and the recalcitrance of the strings, but is there any way to dispel this darkness? I feel sure about the percussion. I feel confident about the strings and the songs when they sweep away the spinning drone in the mouth of the toothless night. Oh, ring forth, my lute! Cleanse my spirit, fiddle! Silence . . . silence. Be kind to my heart, my mute friends, for silence is frightening. When will the strings play some tunes?"

A cold, imaginary chamber and the musical instruments, which are stored in the corners, confront me. There are changing images on the walls. A large one of the Eastern music ensemble includes the five musicians. Musical notes. Images from bygone days. The merchants' coffeehouse. The Suriyan clock. The sailing-barge harbor opposite the date warehouse. The bar known as The White Rose. No one. All the same, the picture of the Eastern music ensemble affords me intense delight and stormy pleasure. I sit on a chair, the chair of the qanun player Harun, and pull out the drawer of the nearby table. The drawer contains medicine bottles and two lenses from dark glasses, all resting atop a picture of a rural bridge over a grassy creek. The dead kerosene heater is in a corner. There are garments on the coat rack. An ancient candlestick. A fiddle, a lute, a drum, and a cello. I move to an inner room, where there are two bed frames without mattresses, and then to the room opposite, where there are also empty bedsteads and leftover tins of food. I return to the small, central chamber and gaze at the picture of the five musicians. The camera caught them when the excitement of finishing a heart-rending song had overwhelmed them. They were holding the necks of their instruments affectionately and delightedly. The picture is many years old.

There is no one here. I turn my head to the gaps of the windows of the wooden balcony, which is connected to the parlor. The luminous moon is close by, adjacent to the windows. Numerous lunar eyes gaze at the silent strings. I descend the stairs after locking the door behind me with the antique key. When I reach the alley, the strings resume playing, and the strange tune is repeated with its melodies and beats, in a sequence with quick passages and adagio ones, falling and rising, in unison and in solos.

What a creative composition this is! It is produced by the radiant solitude, the great heart of the night, and the night's spirit, which is packed with hope, life, and constancy. The song flies through space. The instruments are flying. The musicians are flying, as in a painting by Chagall. I walk along the empty streets, tipsy with an excess of emotions inspired by Orpheus. The city repeats the song. The city is dancing. It strips itself to fly. The dead emerge from the netherworld and share in the singing.

Four Points of Entry
to Basrayatha

The distance between the city and the man was no longer even a wall's span.

Paul Éluard

You will find no new lands, you will find no other seas.
The city will follow you. You will roam the same
streets. And you will age in the same neighborhoods;
and you will grow gray in these same houses.
Always you will arrive in this city. Do not hope for any other—
There is no ship for you, there is no road.
As you have destroyed your life here
in this little corner, you have ruined it in the entire world.

Constantine Cavafy

1

The Loom and the Rostrum

NARRATORS RECOUNT THE bygone events and marvels of ancient cities, but in Basrayatha I recount what is known and recorded in the lines of destiny. Not everything there is marvelous. What is amazing, though, is the power of every citizen in it and a veracity that surpasses any other power. When you are in a mood to marvel, you must inevitably find that what is widespread and common in the natures and customs of nations is marvelous, rare, and unparalleled. Al-Asma'i, for example, told of a palm tree that rats climbed in order to eat its dates. Al-Jahiz sketched a scene of crows covering the crowns of palm trees, which had caught fire, in order to glean culls remaining among the stumps of branches and the palm's fibers, even though these birds would not approach ripening clusters of dates. Al-Nabahani, al-Qazwini, and Shahrazad narrated other marvels concerning the land and the sea. I will add to these tales of loving coexistence by tracing the fragmented destinies of creatures from the past and the present.

Back when these marvels were daily fleeting sights, there was nothing amazing about them, except for their inevitable transformation in the telling. The events and scenes of our times have been waiting for that power of amazement to envelop and take hold of

167

them for our mouths, ears, and minds. We are no longer satisfied with the limitations of a fleeting incident or the transient simplicity of a scene. Instead we spread the wings of doubt and the hand of interpretation to wrap these in the carpet of magic and disguise. The narrator conceals what was obvious in the scene and reveals what was hidden in it. He turns it upside down like an expert conjurer who—to seduce his audience—is impelled to ever greater feats of enticement and bafflement. In the imagination of each follower is born a storyteller who receives from his predecessor the ceremonial staff of storytelling and who influences the senses and intellects of those following him until the matter almost surpasses the bounds of narration to become literary fiction and goes from commercial entertainment to the power of amazement. Thus none of us can imagine a city without a storyteller or a storyteller without a rostrum, which may resemble the hump of a camel, the prow of a ship, or the edge of a mirage. This characteristic became so common in Basrayatha that no one could any longer imagine that a city could develop without a storyteller or a rostrum, anywhere on earth . . . whether with a single rostrum and many storytellers or a single storyteller and many rostra . . . for a single scene with many visages . . . or a single visage with fluctuating scenes. So this city has no history until time clothes it with the cloak of events. You begin its history wherever you wish by pulling from its cloak a thread with which to weave an incident or a narrative. For this reason, its history has not begun yet. It could have begun at the time the astrologers appointed for its passing, no matter how it began or ended. I cannot imagine in Basrayatha a storyteller without a rostrum or a citizen without a loom. The rostrum and the loom are the secret emblems of this city.

2

Before I Was Born, If I Truly Was Born

Before cities existed, there were stakes and ruins left by foreigners, blind travelers, and prophets. Before cities, their traces, plans, names, and passing thoughts were in the air. Then the architects of the cities were born. Before Troy there was the *Iliad*, which attracted Homer's staff to it, so that he recited his epic narrative to bring Troy into existence. Before the serpent, there was immortal life. Then came Gilgamesh, who defended Uruk. Immortality is the origin of Uruk. An epic quest attracted Gilgamesh. Uruk was a thought waiting beneath the serpent's skin. Before the palm tree, the fruit and the seed existed. Once the date palm came into existence, it needed an enclosure. The walled enclosure asked to be filled with houses, and Basrayatha came into existence. Before Basra, there was Basrayatha. Had it not been for the date palm, there would have been no baskets for harvesting dates. Had there been no baskets for harvesting dates, there would have been no date pickers. Had there been no date pickers, there would have been no ships. Had there been no ships, there would have been no port. Had there been no port, no city would have been built. Al-Jahiz roamed through the markets of the ancient city and stood in front of a bench in a mosque, where he heard the conversations of East Africans, the South Asian Jats, and ordinary citizens as a buzz, which he distinguished from the language of the Arabs. Were it not for the common folk, the ports would not have come into existence. If it were not for the grammatical errors of diverse groups of people, the Arabic language would not have come into existence. If this language had not come into existence, there would have been no letter 'ayn or its mate. If not for his book *The Misers*, al-Jahiz would not have existed, and had there been no misers to discuss, there would have been no authors. And without them we would not have existed. Without all of us, there would be no cities. There was someone resembling me among those people of mixed background. He rubbed shoulders with al-Jahiz and composed the book *Basrayatha*. He lived the book before me. Someone unknown to me would have written it, had he not sent it to my address, which would not have existed had there been no city, harbor, river, ship, palm tree, date, seed, or immortality. This order may also be reversed, descending to the date or ascending to a firebrand: the journey of existence . . . the existence that precedes existing entities . . . the succession that engendered my book before I was born and that begat me before Basrayatha was born.

Basrayatha certainly would not have been born had I not generated its plans in this book. The book's essence appeared from nonexistence to grant a name to a newborn fully aware of its own birth, since its birth was repeated over and over again. As rough as a rock, as delicate as a freshly ripe date, as briny as well water, as sweet as spring water, it settled before an author to complete his creation, which the hands of previous creators had repeatedly molded from unnamed, ancient, original elements. The book and the author were not one, two, or ten. They did not cease to exist and thus resembled the unripe date traveling in the womb of Basrayatha—that sacred, fertile, vaginal opening. So the book gave birth to itself, from itself.

I do not know if I was born previously, but when Basrayatha was born, I must necessarily have existed within her. How amazing! How I could be inside her and also travel toward her at the same time:

her son and a stranger all at once. I am not a hypocrite; Gilgamesh also traveled without ever leaving Uruk. His plight resembles that of travelers to Basrayatha in one of my stories. Should I discredit my own testimony and believe my dream or should I believe myself and deny my dream? Or are the dream, the trip, and the composition all aspects of a single, indivisible existence? Which of the routes to Basrayatha is the shortest? This is an essential question. Anyone who answers it correctly receives a *laissez-passer* to the city before all others.

I want my book to pave the way for the stories that come after it, but are its chapters not a part of the stories that have preceded it? That is the way it is, for if it had existed before Basrayatha, it would have been fated to be published at any time prior to the moment of this publication. I do not know when my book was born. Even if I knew when it was written, I do not know when it will die. This book will also age, and must inevitably make a return trip to its grave. When the book dies, its author will be forgotten, for his lifespan is linked to his book's, and Basrayatha will die if its book dies.

3

Utopias and Heterotopias

What is referred to as a cultural survey of a contemporary city captures in miniature the anarchy of existence. I can find no rationale for locating obstetric hospitals near cemeteries, an amusement park near a house of worship, a prison near a school, a garden next to the desert, or a palace next to a shack in a city layout that is surrounded by a single wall or connected by roads intersecting in one plane, unless this plan is a symbolic, dialectical representation of two contrary types of creative discourse. Our evolution from one city to another is our movement from one model to another. In every part of the world, cities are nothing but repeated examples of a single, dialectical prototype.

No road will ever lead you to a destination other than one of these two: here or there. They are symbols for two worlds on a horizontal plane consisting of the beginning, the beginning revisited, or the beginning repeated. The situation will be no better in a model city, where we assume that representative stratified classes, which are composed of harmonious elements, substitute for the horizontal plane of disharmonious elements, because moving up or down between these strata will never mean anything more than our movement from a harmonious layer to a disharmonious one (or the opposite): from above to below or vice versa, even if our planet grows crowded with hundreds of clusters of these stacked, cylindrical cities. That is the circumscribing limit of our real existence in any place. Our initial existence somewhere is the beginning of creation. Our transfer to another place is the continuation of creation, not its renewal. No matter how many times we repeat it, we will not prolong our existence. We persevere in existence but do not change it. We are ourselves anywhere in the world. Our consciousness of this truth inspires us to travel to a placeless place, to a utopia on another plane of existence, but the possibility that this time-delimited existence will end prompts us to seek only to exist in one place, because a single existence does not differ from multiple similar ones, and the latter do not nullify the former. Even if the two differ in location, they are composed alike and are in sequence with each other.

The goal of the ancient thinker was to establish cities that were peaceful, harmonious, and linked to the human soul's four virtues: wisdom, courage, temperance, and justice. In fact, the ultimate goal of constructing a model city like Plato's Republic was to explore or to search for the fourfold health of the soul. Whether occurring as wars, natural disasters, revolutions, popular democracies, oligarchies, spaceships, or robots, natural and man-made realities of existence have put an end to this human dream. The dream has become an uneasy one, and model cities have become unfinished projects for anxious souls and weary imaginations. The tragedy of modern man is that he will not be able to build cities based on the plans of ancient ones. No longer will cities that open onto bordering plains, deserts, and oceans—like Athens, Sparta, Basra, Kufa, Wasit, Baghdad, Isfahan, Herat, Carthage, Rome, New York, and Brasilia—be built. City planners today are content with gigantic, hyper-quantified plans that allow no room for human error—even on the magnitude of one to a million—to creep in. They use these to erect building clusters lodged between earth and sky. Their dream-absorbing realms prevent travel through their skies.

Has the human dream come to an end? The dream of Odysseus on the coast of Ithaca? Penelope's dream that Odysseus would return? The death of the ancient cities has not bequeathed to us any dream of the ancient storyteller besides his Penelopean dynamic: that we weave our stories by night to unravel them the next day.

Since the ascending road is also the descending one, I have pictured Basrayatha as two cities, in both of which I have existed at the same time. When I am inside one of them, I am outside it at the very same time. I had my own ways of arguing this paired feeling before I read what Michel Foucault had to say about heterotopias.* I only made this discovery recently, but he has furnished me with a new argument.

---

* Michel Foucault, "Of Other Spaces (1967), Heterotopias," posted online as of October 12, 2005 at http://foucault.info/documents/heteroTopia/foucault.heteroTopia.en.html. (T)

According to Foucault's definition, the city is a collection of spaces (or sites or locations) that share relationships and contradictory characteristics with other spaces that reflect the original spaces and that perform dissimilar functions (raising doubts, diverting, and turning upside down). Foucault distinguishes between two classes of these dissimilar spaces. The first are utopias, which have no physical location. The second are heterotopias, which grant space to the spaceless in the heart of the actual space. A simple version of a heterotopia is the mirror, in which—from our actual location before it—we see our existence in reverse. The more complicated and varied versions, which all human civilizations without exception have shared in establishing, are set forth by Foucault as falling into five main types described according to five principles.

The first principle distinguishes between two types of heterotopias. There are crisis heterotopias, which include random geographical sites that are reserved, sanctified, or restricted. These are dedicated to a group of adolescents, to menstruating or pregnant women, to the elderly or to other persons in a state of crisis vis-à-vis their society. Boarding schools, army barracks, and honeymoon hotels are examples of heterotopias of crisis. The second type is the deviant heterotopia, where individuals whose conduct is characterized as deviating from the norm are crammed together, as, for example, in rest homes, mental hospitals, prisons, and retirement communities.

The second principle classifies a type of heterotopia performing a function different from its original one. The heterotopia referred to as a cemetery, for example, may be a sacred or eternal space for a city but may also evolve into an alternative city, where each family possesses a darkened place of rest.

The third principle is that heterotopias may bring together in one physical space a number of different and incompatible spaces. Theater, cinema, public garden, and zoo are examples of this phenomenon. "The garden is the smallest parcel of the world and then it is the totality of the world."*

The fourth principle corresponds to the fourth type of heterotopia, which is the temporal one: towers composed of time-segments, which stack endlessly atop a single location. This could be a public archive like a library or a museum. Another, contrary type of heterotopia either eradicates time or leads to a rediscovery of time—for example, sporting competitions and festivals.

The fifth principle provides a type of heterotopia that is based on an open-and-shut system by which a heterotopia is both open to everyone and also segregated. Thus there are exposed but isolated heterotopias like a guest room that is isolated in a home away from the family's living quarters or as in a motel away from other guest rooms. On the basis of this principle, radical heterotopias have been established: brothels and colonies. Foucault finally arrived at the seaborne type of heterotopia: the ship. This type includes not only ships devoted to exploration and economic development but also the adventurer's treasure ship. "The ship is the heterotopia par excellence. In civilizations without boats, dreams dry up, espionage takes the place of adventure, and the police take the place of pirates."†

Where shall I begin a comparison of the different types of heterotopias? I feel that the summary of Foucault's principles greatly weakens any attempt to draw inferences from the model cities of the Arab East. If I begin with the final type mentioned by Foucault— the ship—in order to compare it to the train, which is a mobile

---

* Ibid. (T)
† Ibid. (T)

city, I find that each is a great storehouse for the imagination and a way to travel toward cities lacking any real existence except as mirrors of real places. The train reflects a utopia that deserves another, heterotopian name. This is Basrayatha, which reaches into the heart of the real space of Iraq just as al-Farabi's Virtuous City contained parallels to the ignorant, wayward, erring, noble, vile, conquering, beautiful, and the licentious cities. The cities of al-Ma'arri, al-Suhrawardi, Ibn Sina, and Ibn Tufayl similarly shone with a sequence of mirrored reflections terminating in a single image like Basrayatha. Foucault considered travel by camel, horse, automobile, ship, and bicycle to be expressions of connection to numerous internal heterotopias. This book is the outcome of travel between counterpoised places, whether remote, adjacent, or overlapping: towers and fields that appear in relationship to each other in an orderly fabric like the immortal fabric of a utopia: restricted, sanctified, and favored.

One Basrayathan incarnation became evident during the 1980–1988 war. At that time I conceived of the desert as a heterotopia at the brink of silence outside the city, and that heterotopia took the form of the Camel's Eye. Then visionary heterotopias materialized in narrative types. These were the heterotopias of war, for which this book furnishes a wide-ranging retrospective. When the mirror loses light, descriptions become inoperative and the journey ends. It is not possible to remain in a real place without a journey into the heteropic mirror. Arriving there is a confirmation of the reality of that single real place, which— even if it is the smallest point on the earth—represents the entire earth. Garden, river, desert, and railway stations are happy, miniature worlds.

Another person might travel around the world without settling in any real place. I feel, unlike him, that I am in my place and that the world travels around me.

4

The Permanent Citizen

Socrates lived for seventy years, during which time he left Athens only for war or on some necessary mission. When he was well advanced in years, the Athenians accused him of atheism, of corrupting the minds of the young, and of rebelling against the laws of the state. So he was hauled into court. Socrates did not wish to have his punishment changed from the death penalty pronounced against him to banishment from the city. He also rejected his friends' counsel to escape from prison. Socrates told his judges who asked him to suggest an alternative penalty: "If I say exile . . . I must indeed be blinded by the love of life, if I am so irrational as to expect that when you, who are my own citizens, cannot endure my discourses and words, and have found them so grievous and odious that you will have no more of them, others are likely to endure me. . . . And what a life should I lead, at my age, wandering from city to city, ever changing my place of exile, always driven out! For I am quite sure that wherever I go, there, as here, the young men will flock to me; and if I drive them away, their elders will drive me out at their request; and if I let them come, their fathers and friends will drive me out for their sakes."* Socrates similarly cited his respectful reverence for first principles when refusing his friend Crito's advice to flee from his prison; first and foremost his respect for the laws of Athens. Only a depraved person who repays evil with evil would oppose them. If he fled, he would live, but how? "As the flatterer of all men,

---

* Plato, "Apology," 37 c–e; Benjamin Jowett translation. (T)

and the servant of all men."* What then would have become of those fine sentiments he expressed concerning justice and virtue? The many questions and parables of Socrates are also found in Plato's other dialogues and constitute another ingenious defense conducted through Platonic dialectics. The defense at the trial could not supplant the defense in his previous debates in which the Good was associated with a death joined to spiritual bliss in the Other World. Indeed, there was inevitably another hypothesis, which was derived from a hetero-place. It would not have depicted flight as evil, if this escape had been for the sake of continuing his advocacy of virtue and his fight against injustice—both of which Socrates invoked in the trial. Who among us, however, has an inner voice of the kind that Socrates listened to when it advised him what was right, allowing him to argue, on this basis, that death is a lesser evil than flight?

Socrates had an inner guide that directed him to avoid doing any evil. Perhaps Pasternak heard the same inner voice when he refused voluntary exile from his country after the authorities made him choose between a hard life at home and a free departure from the Soviet Union after he was awarded the Nobel Prize for Literature. Pasternak did not balance exile against death, but said that exile is equivalent to death. This recent example lends strength to the hypothesis that ethical and legal concerns can merge. It lends us the force of its argument to demonstrate the existence of the Good in the Socratic phenomenon of the permanent citizen.

Does the citizen of a modern state require concepts superior to Virtue, Piety, and the Supreme Good; or the liberation of the spirit from the body's fetters; or an absolute, supreme paradigm, in order

---

* Plato, "Crito," 53 e; Benjamin Jowett translation. (T)

to construct a philosophic position comparable to that of Socrates? He said: "The philosopher during his lifetime is fettered by the body's manacles that shackle everyone, but philosophy speaks to him, and he listens to her discourse. So it cleanses him of the base bodily element and removes from his inner vision the emotions' clouds and the senses' deception."*

By taking the gist of the previous paragraph, we will achieve an essential summary of an idea that is appropriate for every time and place. I think the subject does not require any hetero-introduction to the Socratic dichotomies of Piety and Justice, or Revered and Loved, or Ugly and Beautiful, or to his theory about the mutual generation of opposites in order for us to begin deriving new results from old hypotheses. We have little need for strong arguments to prove a hypothesis like this one: the permanent citizen is a righteous one. I think we are fast approaching the gates of Plato's Republic, which itself is also merely one of the consequences of the Socratic theory of forms.

As Bertrand Russell concludes, the Republic is a model, nothing more or less, and "the model remains a model. It is not suggested as a practical plan for setting up an actual city."† I believe that the task of creating a universal picture of a model city may be reduced to defining the existence of a specific, real city. The only role for a lofty model is to lead us to the actual, defective reality. This link is quite close to the mutually generative link between opposites. It possesses an irrefutable, essential dialectic force, because the

---

* Zaki Naguib Mahmoud, from the introduction to his translation of Plato's "Phaedo" in *Muhawirat Aflatun (The Dialogues of Plato)*. (A)
† Bertrand Russell, *Wisdom of the West* (Garden City, New York: Doubleday & Company, Inc., 1959), 66. (A/T)

possibility of exchanging the portrait for the original—the model for the modeled entity—establishes our ability to devise multiple models for ideal cities. The existence of a righteous citizen in an ideal model like the Republic assumes the existence of a counterpart for him in an actual city. While the phrase "permanent citizen" is an appropriate characterization of every citizen in the model city, it becomes appropriate also as a description for some citizens of actual cities. If the permanent citizens of model cities are merely archetypes, then I am inclined to consider them the same in real, actual cities. In other words, they both exist and do not exist at one and the same time. They exist in their individual, material approximation and by the force of law but are merely models that can travel mentally wherever they wish. Citizens of the modern state are warmly urged to take armchair journeys from their place of origin so they can discover its universal truth: its hidden essence.

This is what has led me—a permanent citizen in an actual city, which hides its true nature beneath a heap of fickle history's debris and social tragedies—to rediscover repeatedly my city and to pretend to forget any reality subsequent to it. If my wisdom proves inadequate, as everyone else's wisdom does, including that of Socrates, or if my wisdom is of those types assigned to all human beings,* then I have wrested from myself what humanity possesses here and there of the remaining bits of wisdom that have been able to escape the bonds of a body enervated by remaining in a single place. Similarly, a flood of developments has stolen from it the pure sensation of things. I

---

* In the "Apology" of Plato, Socrates says, in dismissing any special claim to wisdom: "Men of Athens, this reputation of mine has come of a certain sort of wisdom which I possess. If you ask me what kind of a certain sort of wisdom, I reply, wisdom such as may perhaps be attained by man, for to that extent I believe I am wise." Plato, "Apology," 20 d (Jowett translation). (A/T)

have needed a different philosophy and another power of sensation in order to bring light to bear on the life of the city that has caused me to tarry as if I were a prisoner within its walls. Here is what I wrote about this city one day in the year 1987, during the [Iran-Iraq] War: "My preoccupation with this place has caused me to brood more about the extent of the city in which I live and which I have not left for forty-five years, except when forced to do so. I needed a foreign eye to gain definite knowledge about my city—since I was inseparable from it—so that I could discover it. I have denied it so I may know it. I have destroyed it so I could build it—substituting for it a utopia— so I could retain its original truth."

Movement from one position to another, from the particular to the universal, and vice versa, means nothing more than lingering in the same place. There is no contradiction between the image of what is external and what is internal. When you write about the city that you know very well, you distance yourself from it a great deal so it will be nothing more than an image, a memory, or a distant melody into which all tunes flow in a mysterious way. What I have done in this book is in no way superior to the work of any other permanent citizen who thinks as I do and who supports the statement of Heraclitus: "Men do not know how what is at variance agrees with itself. It is the attunement of opposite tensions, like that of the bow and the lyre."*

---

* Quoted in Russell, *Wisdom of the West*, 24. (A/T)

Glossary

abudhiya: rural Iraqi lyric with *–iya* as the ending for every fourth line

Buwayb: a river that runs through Jaykur

Jaykur: a hamlet on the Shatt al-Arab, reasonably close to Basra but near the Iran border

Maude, Sir Frederick Stanley: British commander in Iraq, where he died November 11, 1917

mizmar: Middle Eastern folk clarinet

mubattil: ascetic

muhtasib: official charged with regulating markets

qanun: Middle Eastern zither

qasab: *Phragmites communis*, bamboo-like giant grass (reed, cane) growing over twenty feet tall

rabab: spike fiddle

al-Sayyab, Badr Shakir: influential Iraqi poet who hailed from Jaykur (1926–64) *shami*: fictive currency used in the calculations of Basra's date merchants in the nineteenth century

sidr (or sidir): a tree *(Zizyphus spina Christi)* of the buckthorn family also known as the lote tree or Christ's thorn

slubi: a desert doctor, a Bedouin Christian with claims to Crusader descent

Souk al-Maghayiz: a market for modern shops

Suriyan: Basra resident of Armenian heritage who erected a public clock for the city

Thamud: ancient Arab tribe

Thamudi or Thamudic: referring to the tribe of Thamud and to ancient North Arabian scripts, including Taymanitic (Thamudic A) in which a single letter stands for both dh and z

Zanj: East Africans in Iraq; in Abbasid times some formed a separate military corps, but many were employed removing a salty crust from farmland. They staged a major rebellion against the Abbasid regime